"Unless you've been living in a cave, you know the culture has become more dangerous for kids. As a developmental psychologist and character educator, I don't know of any book that does a better job of documenting those dangers than Marcia Segelstein's *Don't Let the Culture Raise Your Kids.* If you're a parent who wants to raise children to be faith-filled, virtuous, and principled human beings in a society that's increasingly hostile to those values, you won't find a better battle plan than this terrific resource. All of the chapters are packed with parenting strategies, tips, and tools (the recommendations for controlling screens are worth the price of the book). These are backed up by modern science and illustrated with encouraging stories of real families that are pushing back against the culture and raising kids with the conscience and character to resist it. This book is a godsend for families of faith, but it's also for everyone who cares about kids and wants to learn more about how to deal with the very real threats to their hearts, minds, and souls from the world they now have to grow up in. Consider it for a book study in your church, school, or community — and offer a copy to your pastor. Bravo! to Marcia Segelstein for writing it."

– Thomas Lickona, director, Center for the 4th and 5th Rs
(Respect and Responsibility), State University of New York
at Cortland, and author of *How to Raise Kind Kids: And Get
Respect, Gratitude, and a Happier Family in the Bargain*

"Parents trying to limit today's cultural influences on their children can find a wealth of information in Marcia Segelstein's well-researched book. Written with journalistic thoroughness, she sheds light on the issues and trends that justifiably cause parents to be concerned for the health, safety, and spiritual well-being of their kids. Not just that, Marcia also offers concrete suggestions to battle the culture's impact while building stronger Christian families. For parents in the trenches, this is a must-read."

– Marybeth Hicks, speaker, author,
columnist, and radio host

Don't Let the Culture Raise Your Kids

MARCIA SEGELSTEIN

Don't Let the
Culture
Raise Your
Kids

Our Sunday Visitor

www.osv.com
Our Sunday Visitor Publishing Division
Our Sunday Visitor, Inc.
Huntington, Indiana 46750

Our Sunday Visitor Publishing Division
Our Sunday Visitor, Inc.
200 Noll Plaza
Huntington, IN 46750
1-800-348-2440

ISBN: 978-1-68192-276-8 (Inventory No. T1962)
eISBN: 978-1-68192-277-5
LCCN: 2018968557

Cover and interior design: Lindsey Riesen
Cover art: Photo by Paul Hanaoka on Unsplash

PRINTED IN THE UNITED STATES OF AMERICA

For Katie and Jack

TABLE OF CONTENTS

INTRODUCTION

Writing this book from the perspective of a journalist, I've drawn on the lessons learned in covering family-related issues, first as a television news producer, and then as a writer. But there's no question that my work — and this book — have been influenced by having children of my own and experiencing the challenges of raising them in our current culture.

Despite believing that I was vigilant as a mother, I was taken by surprise many times by what my children experienced, what they were exposed to, and even what they were explicitly taught in school. I wasn't prepared for the onslaught of cultural messages that were directly opposed to the Christian beliefs, morals, and values I was trying to instill.

With that said, this book is not a guide to "how to raise your children like I did." I have made far too many mistakes for that! This book is about what I learned after digging into issues that took on added importance because I was a mother — it's the book I wish I was given when I became a mom.

I first started covering family issues as a producer for *CBS This Morning*. The "Family Time" segment I produced reported on issues including divorce and its impact on children, childcare, early childhood education, family health, adolescence, work/family balance, the importance of fathers, aging — almost anything relating to families and kids.

After my daughter was born and I left CBS News to be a full-time mother, I began to write from home on those same issues, eventually becoming a senior editor for *Salvo* magazine and writing for the *National Catholic Register.* The topics I've covered range from the impact of pornography on children and teens, to the work of Dr. Miriam Grossman on the untruths of contemporary sex education in public schools, to the enormous influence on kids of both the culture and their peers, thanks to social media — to name a few.

Everything I've learned through my research and writing has provided the impetus for this book. I want to share what I've learned about the outsized influence the culture has on raising our kids, and what Christian parents can do to take back their families.

When I was growing up, the culture might not have been explicitly Christian, but it didn't actively work against Christian morality and values, either. Today it does. If Christian parents want to stop this trend — especially before it gets worse — they need to think and act differently. Unfortunately, modern parents are often ill-equipped to do this because it isn't only children who are negatively influenced by the culture: parents are, too. It's easy to feel alone and insecure when you're the only parent setting limits on screen time, or refusing to buy the latest tech gadget, or pulling your child out of sex ed class. It's easy to feel like the "bad guy" when other parents are acting like their children's friends.

For both parents and children, the cultural onslaughts are pervasive. Educators take it upon themselves to school students in culturally correct notions of gender, sex, and marriage. The click of a mouse or the touch of a smartphone can expose children to obscene pornographic images. The entertainment and advertising industries seem hell-bent on destroying childhood innocence and ramping up a propensity for materialism, to say nothing of promiscuity. With the pervasiveness of technology and social media, peers often replace parents as the primary influence in a child's life.

Our goal as Christian parents is to guide our children toward heaven. That's not where they'll be directed if we let the culture raise our kids. This book will show you how to be the parents your children need. You'll learn how to lead your children with confidence and authority. You'll discover where the pitfalls lie and just how dangerous the world can be for kids. But more importantly, you'll acquire the skills needed to protect them from the many dangerous lies-disguised-as-truth that can lure them away from you, and away from the Faith.

CHAPTER 1

THE CRITICAL ROLE
OF PARENTS

During my years of writing about child raising, the one issue that has stood out above all others has been the changing role of parents. The doctors, therapists, and researchers I've interviewed, and the studies I've read, all seem to agree on two key points: First, modern parents are abdicating their role as authority figures. Second, children *desperately need* their parents to be authority figures.

The culture has shifted away from one that not only accepted, but encouraged "strict" parenting, to one that sees that word in a negative, even mocking light.

"Permissive parenting" was popularized in the 1970s. Today's version is "positive parenting." Modern parents are advised to affirm their children and avoid correcting them; they're encouraged to be their children's friends; they're warned not to stifle their children's creativity. "Discipline" now smacks of negativity. All of these make it that much more difficult for parents trying to raise children of faith, which requires both respectfulness and self-discipline. Not only can Christian parents feel as though they're swimming against the tide, they can feel like they're doing it alone.

Yet, I would venture to guess that if you were to ask most parents today — even very young parents — whether they would ever have dreamed of speaking to their parents the way their children talk to them (or the way they see other children interact with their parents), the answer would be a resounding "No!" I'm also guessing that most of us have witnessed children misbehaving in places such as restaurants, movie theaters, or other public spaces and cringed while their parents said and did nothing.

Have you ever imagined what happens when undisciplined tots become teenagers? Young children who don't respect the authority of their parents don't grow into adolescents who suddenly do. They'll turn to the world, to their peers — as they're hormonally inclined to do anyway — to decide what's right and wrong. If parents don't address this, they're affirming the behavior.

You've already made the decision to raise your children as faithful Christians. That means you're going to have to guide them through a world that actively works against that goal. The task ahead of you is daunting, but manageable. We live in a culture that condones abortion, mocks chastity, embraces gender fluidity, and devalues marriage. We live in a world where children and adolescents are increasingly more connected to their peers than their parents, particularly thanks to social media. We live in a time when educators teach politically correct values, not biblical ones.

If we want our children to follow us, instead of the culture, we need to gain their respect. We need our children to listen to us and to trust us, so that ours are the values they embrace, and ours are the voices they heed.

That means the first task is to become confident, authoritative parents.

What Being an Authority Means (and Why It Matters)

We associate authority with being stern, rigid, and tough. It is tempting to think of this as old-fashioned and unnecessary but being an authority figure for our children means being

in charge. Plain and simple. It means being able to say "No."
It absolutely does *not* preclude being nurturing, caring, and
loving. In fact, these are critical elements to being an effective authority figure.

Dr. Jane Anderson practiced as a pediatrician for thir-
ty-five years and is now a Clinical Professor of Pediatrics
at the University of California San Francisco. She's also on
the Board of Directors for the American College of Pediatricians. In an interview for the *National Catholic Register*, I
asked her if authority is an important component of parenting. "It's crucial. It's the foundation of family. It's the foundation of society," she answered. "Authoritative parents are
closest to the biblical concept of parents. These are parents
who provide rules, provide standards — usually high standards — for their children. But they're nurturing, responsive
and loving. I call them the nurturing, loving, rule-setting
parents."[1] Children raised by authoritative parents consistently have the best outcomes on a wide range of measures.[2]

In fact, as noted by the American College of Pediatricians, authoritative parenting is a specific style recognized
by pediatricians and child psychologists as being the ideal.[3]
By contrast, *permissive* parents are reluctant to set rules and
standards, while *authoritarian* parents are demanding, lack
warmth, and are unresponsive to their children.

Anderson believes that as children learn to respect the
authority of their parents, they learn to respect authority in
society. More importantly, if children don't acknowledge the
authority of their parents, why should they believe that God
has authority over them?

Just Can't Say "No!"
William Doherty is director of the Marriage and Family
Therapy Program at the University of Minnesota. In his
book, *Take Back Your Kids: Confident Parenting in Turbulent
Times*, he talks about the disrespect and general coarseness
common among the children and teenagers with whom he

works. A big part of the problem is the unwillingness of parents to put limits on their children. He writes that the best research indicates that "children need both love and limits, they need confident rather than insecure parents."[4]

Part of the discomfort the present parenting culture has with authority is rooted in what Doherty calls "therapeutic parenting." He writes that starting with the publication in the 1970s of Thomas Gordon's *Parent Effectiveness Training: The Tested New Way to Raise Responsible Children*, parents have been repeatedly told to behave like therapists with their children. Among other things, this means being non-judgmental and constantly attentive. A therapeutic culture of parenting will distort parents' interactions with their child, presuming that a child's psyche must be treated gingerly, and can lead to what Doherty calls "timid parent syndrome."[5] When Johnny kicks Mommy, Mommy tries to use it as a "teachable moment." When Johnny's teacher is unhappy with his behavior or school performance, Mommy acts as if it's the teacher's fault. Child psychologist Ron Taffel describes the plight of a mother he once counseled: When her six-year-old son hit her and screamed at her in a store, she wasn't sure whether she should "smack him on the spot or let him get his feelings off of his chest so they wouldn't fester."[6] Doherty recounts treating a family in therapy whose ten-year-old had begun calling his mother a "bitch." He believes issues such as these are due to the widespread blurring of the boundaries between parents and children.

Another expectation put on modern parents is that they shouldn't interfere with their children's desire to express themselves. "The parents who don't say no to their children will tell you they don't want to stifle the child's creativity. But that's exactly what they're doing by not saying no," Dr. Anderson told me. "Unless a child has experienced someone saying no, that child does not have to think creatively or problem solve."[7]

Besides ceding the role of authority figures, modern parenting has changed in other ways. For one thing, children are catered to in a way they were not in previous generations. "You see it with the hyper-praising of kids, particularly middle-class kids, who are given the message that every time they breathe they're a little genius. Parents will bend over backwards," Doherty told me in an interview for *Salvo* magazine, "to make sure their kids have the most special birthday party, for example."[8] As a result, children develop an inflated sense of entitlement beginning in their early years.

It reminds me of the story Texas mom Kay Wills Wyma tells in her book, *Cleaning House: A Mom's 12-Month Experiment to Rid Her Home of Youth Entitlement*. Her moment of truth came while driving her fourteen-year-old son to school. Pointing out two luxury cars nearby, he asked her which one she thought he'd look better in. Taken aback, she thought to herself, "Who's raising this kid?" She realized that her children had no real responsibilities, no appreciation for hard work, and an outsized sense of entitlement. And it was her doing. Her children expected their beds to be made for them, their dirty laundry to be washed, dinner to be on the table every night — and yet they didn't know how to do any of those things themselves. She spent the next year redefining her approach to raising her five children by giving each of them regular responsibilities and assigning them specific chores.

Like children, parents are not immune from peer pressure. Doherty tells the story of a four-year-old who suddenly demanded that her mother hang her coat up after arriving at preschool one day. "The girl had never done this before, but had obviously seen other kids treat their parents as servants." The mother firmly told her child to hang it up herself. Later a teacher remarked that she was the first parent who'd handled such a situation that way.[9]

Letting the Kids Decide

Dr. Leonard Sax, a pediatrician and psychologist with years of hands-on experience and loads of research conducted all over the world, has weighed in on the topic of parental authority. For him, it's not just a matter of parents abdicating their authority. He believes that "letting the kids decide" has become the new mantra of what's considered "good" parenting, especially in the U.S.

In his book, *The Collapse of Parenting: How We Hurt Our Kids When We Treat Them Like Grown-Ups*, Sax writes that basic parental functions, such as teaching right from wrong, are often ignored. Sax believes that part of the problem is that parents used to be able to count on schools to help in this area. Early childhood educators have shifted their focus away from teaching life lessons about good and bad behavior in exchange for a focus on academics. For one thing, as Sax notes, schools avoid controversy when they teach straightforward subjects like math and stay away from instruction about right and wrong. Another part of the problem, Sax asserts, is when winning their children's love and affection becomes the primary focus of the parents. "Too often, parents today allow their desire to please their child to govern their parenting." Children need parents with the confidence and authority to teach right from wrong, to make rules, and to enforce them, says Sax.[10]

Cautionary Tales

Taffel uses the phrase "the new anger" to describe an upsurge in outrageous behavior by children, and he reports that in his experience it's "becoming the norm in ordinary families."[11] In his book *Childhood Unbound*, he tells the story of "Jessica," who has been told by her mother to turn off the TV and clean up the table. "'Not now,' Jessica says, without bothering to look up. 'No, Jessica, I mean this minute,' her mother says sharply. 'Later,' Jessica responds, almost absentmindedly. Mom stiffens and threatens: 'Stop it now, or there won't be TV tonight.' Finally, she's got her daughter's attention. Jessica looks her mother squarely in the face and says, 'F--- you, Mommy!' Jessica is eight years old."[12]

In addition to lack of respect, there are behaviors that

were unthinkable only a few years ago. Another story Taffel recounts is that of "Margaret" and her daughter, "Lauren."[13] Margaret considered herself the kind of mom Lauren could talk to, unlike her own parents. And Lauren obliged, telling her mother stories about her friends, while Margaret shared tales of her strict upbringing. "Then one day she came home and found her fourteen-year-old daughter in the bathtub having sex with two boys," Taffel writes. The savvy Lauren maintained her cool, telling her mother she must have imagined they were having sex because of her own strict parents. "Besides, there were bubbles in the tub — how could you know what was really going on?" Taffel reports that for a split-second Margaret almost bought it. Then, coming to her senses, she screamed at her daughter, "What do you think I am — a damn fool?" "Yes," Lauren answered flatly.

During therapy, Taffel learned much that Margaret, the cool, you-can-talk-to-me mom, didn't know about her daughter. Lauren smoked pot, she and her friends all engaged in sex, and she lied about it all in a completely "non-conflicted" way.

Taffel believes that many of today's parents have willfully chosen not to be authoritative, believing that to do so would mean "squelching" their kids. In *Take Back Your Kids*, Doherty recounts what happened when he along with his wife and two kids visited friends whom they hadn't seen since the birth of their daughter, now five-year-old Tanya. After about five minutes of adult conversation, he writes, Tanya "burst into the room and angrily confronted her parents. She said that there was too much 'adult talk' going on and that it was not fun for her. Her parents jolted to attention as if responding to a commanding officer." They apologized to Tanya for their insensitivity, and her mother left to go play with her. "My own children, ages eleven and thirteen at the time, watched this scene with quiet amazement. I don't think they had ever encountered this combination of an autocratic child and timid parents."[14] Taffel describes a scene he witnessed while attending one of his son's softball games. When a kindergartner named Chrissie was declared "out" by the umpire, the child screamed, "I hate you!" and kicked him hard in the shins three times. "Incredibly, her mother, who was watching, did not reprimand her. The umpire did not kick her out of the game, and a few minutes later, Chrissie received the weekly achievement certificate she'd 'earned' — a red ribbon for her participation."[15]

Imagine Chrissie's teammates and the lessons they learned from watching her bad behavior go unpunished. And the grown-ups? Parents who would have handled the situation differently might feel hesitant to be the first to "make a scene" if their children misbehaved. Again, parents are susceptible to peer pressure, too.

Trying Times with Teens

Doherty believes another myth of therapeutic parenting is that parents have little control over their teenagers' behavior. On top of that is the belief that teens *should* make their own decisions so that their development isn't stifled. In *Take Back Your Kids*, he writes, "This myth comes into full play in the later years of high school, by which point many parents have completed the process of resigning as parents and become full-fledged buddies to their children. Thus, half the high-school seniors in town I know of spend their spring break, unchaperoned and with parents' permission, at Mexican frolics that put them at risk for acting out sexually and drinking and abusing drugs. Some of these parents also reserve hotel rooms for their teenagers after the prom, knowing that sexual activity is thereby more likely to occur."[16] Anecdotally, there are endless stories of parents of high schoolers who host parties where the parents either provide the beer, or willfully look the other way while alcohol is being consumed. They're the "cool" parents who make it that much harder for others who want to do very "uncool" things, such as call ahead before parties to be sure the parents will be home and that alcohol won't be served.

Dr. Kathleen Kline is an academic child psychiatrist and affiliate scholar with the Institute for American Values. "Part of adolescent growth is a search for risk-taking, novelty-seeking, and peer affiliation," she told me in an interview for *Salvo*. "It's a very risky time, across millennia."[17] What's changed, she believes, is the environment, specifically an environment rife with technology that can leave parents out of the mix and is potentially toxic for kids.

Losing Influence

Thanks to smartphones, tablets, and computers that facilitate emailing, texting, and instant messaging, instantaneous communication with peers is not only possible, it's become part and parcel of being a child. Gone are the days when households had one or two telephones, and parents knew who was calling their children. Without even having to leave the house, children at younger and younger ages spend vast amounts of time with what Taffel calls their "second family," i.e., their peers. As a result, peer influence plays a much larger role in the lives of modern children. As Dr. Kline told me, "It used to be that parents probably had a pretty good idea who their son or daughter talked to on the way home from school. And if they thought someone was a bad influence, they told their child to stay away from them."[18] There have always been plenty of bad influences within peer groups. Thanks to the digital age, it's difficult for parents to know who their children are talking to or who the bad influences are. Nor do they have any idea of the extent to which their children are being impacted. As Doherty put it, "The amount of screen time kids have [sic] has to dilute parental influence. The use of social media has drastically increased and has got to edge out some parental influence."

Here's how Taffel describes this brave new world children inhabit: "They have an all-access pass to the infinite reach of the internet and are exposed at ever-earlier ages to categories of sex and violence that post-boomer and boomer parents learned about much, much later in life. Cellphones, texting, and online networks afford kids endless freedom in socializing, breaking the old bounds of school and of town. ... The loss of the town center with its eyes and ears — meaning shopkeepers, church and community groups, and school — has left children of all ages more scheduled, but much less policed by the adult world."[19]

Taffel reports reading "astonishingly explicit" text messages from children in elementary and middle school. Unlike small town neighborhoods of the 1950s, which contained the watchful eyes of neighbors and other parents, today's kids can "virtually" hang out with whomever they choose. And that can mean almost anyone on the planet. Thanks to the internet, devices such as smartphones and tablets, and social media, they have access to influences that can be difficult for parents to know about, much less censor.

Dr. Kline was the principal investigator for a study published in 2003 called *Hardwired to Connect: The New Scientific Case for Authoritative Communities.* Sponsored by the YMCA of the USA, Dartmouth Medical School, and the Institute for American Values, it concluded that human beings are "hardwired," i.e. biologically programmed, for connection with other people and with the transcendent. Regarding connections to other people, the report suggests that the answer lies in "authoritative communities," of which the family is first and foremost. "Authoritative" is defined as "warm and involved, but also firm in establishing guidelines, limits, and expectations." As to the need for connection to the transcendent, the study issues this warning:

> Denying or ignoring the spiritual needs of adolescents may end up creating a void in their lives that either devolves into depression or is filled by other forms of questing and challenge, such as drinking, unbridled consumerism, petty crime, sexual precocity, or flirtations with violence. [20]

Even from a purely scientific, secular point of view, there's evidence that children need God! We've already decided on that path. Parents must exert the authority and influence to get our children there.

In his book *The Collapse of Parenting*, Sax cites Dr. Gordon Neufeld, a Canadian psychologist who has been observing children and adolescents for the last forty years. Here's how Neufeld sums up the outsized role peers have assumed: "For the first time in history young people are turning for instruction, modeling, and guidance not to mothers, fathers, teachers, and other responsible adults but to people whom nature never intended to place in a parenting role — their own peers. ... Children are being brought up by immature persons who cannot possibly guide them to maturity. They are being brought up by each other."[21] Sax adds that most kids care more about the esteem of their peers than their parents.

Of course, a huge factor in all of this is technology. The more time a child spends connecting with friends, Sax contends, the more likely he or she will turn to them for guidance about what matters and what doesn't. The contemporary culture of Instagram, Snapchat, and YouTube, or whatever social media sites are most trendy for kids at any given moment, promotes what Sax calls the "premature transfer of allegiance to same-age peers."[22]

The bottom line is that Sax believes that the defiance and disrespect so evident among young people stems from a lack of attachment between parents and kids, which is related to parents abdicating their roles as authority figures. Neufeld puts it this way: "[T]he waning of adult authority is directly related to the weakening of attachments with adults and their displacement by peer attachments."[23]

Sax wrote his book because he believes that the combination of timid parents, along with the hyper-connectedness social media provides, is allowing teenagers to develop their primary attachments to their peers, not their families. Not only do they turn to their peers for guidance about what matters, they seek out approval and love from them. The problem with this, Sax writes, is that parents love their children unconditionally. Peers do not. It's a recipe for disaster.

It seems that a perfect storm of weak, confused parents, and technology with the potential to destroy childhood innocence and redouble peer influence, has come together to create a culture that wreaks havoc on childhood.

SOLUTIONS, TIPS, & TOOLS

Start Young

Dr. Anderson advises parents that when their child is between twelve and fifteen months old, it's time for a transition, and that it's no longer their job to keep their child happy all the time. Up to then, she says, parents try to keep their child smiling and avoid disappointment and frustration at any cost, because, as she puts it, "that's what you do for a baby." But by the age of one, and definitely by two, parents need to change that. Usually at such young ages, "no's" are necessary for safety issues — you can't have your child touching hot stoves or climbing on tables. By fifteen months the "no's" are often necessary for behaviors such as biting, kicking, and hitting. Parents must be prepared to say "no," and to expect their child to be disappointed, frustrated, and unhappy. When that happens, says Anderson, the child has to start problem solving and thinking creatively. Far from stifling creativity or inhibiting their child, parents are actually enhancing and encouraging their child's development when they say "no." They're also teaching diligence, self-reliance, and patience to their children.[24]

If You Didn't Start Young, Start Now

Dr. Den Trumbull is a founding member of the American College of Pediatricians and has been in practice for over thirty years. I asked him about parents who realize they need to change direction, take charge, and become more authoritative. "I want to make it really clear that it's never too late to start," he told me in an interview for *National Catholic Register*. Trumbull suggests that parents begin by choosing two or three behaviors that need work. "Then sit down with your four or six or eight-year-old and apologize. 'We're sorry for how we have mismanaged a, b and c. Because of our love for you we're now going to change our approach, and you're probably not going to be happy with it. But we're doing this for your own good because we realize we've been too easy, too lenient. We've allowed you to do things we shouldn't have. We love you very much, but we need to change our approach.'"[25] Chances are the misbehavior will increase for the first week, Dr. Trumbull says. But generally speaking, after the first week parents will begin to see results.

Rule-making

When making rules, be sure they're clear and age-appropriate. Don't *ask* children to follow rules, *tell* them. And, adds Dr. Sax, don't negotiate. Very young children don't need lengthy explanations about the "whys" behind rules. With older kids, understanding the "whys" will help them take ownership of the rules.

Dr. Thomas Lickona, often called "the father of modern character development," is a developmental psychologist and author of several books, including *How to Raise Kind Kids and Get Respect, Gratitude, and a Happier Family in the Bargain*. He offers some examples of clear and specific rules parents can make:

- "Say 'please' when you'd like something and 'thank you' whenever someone does something for you."

- "Don't interrupt."

- "Look at the person who's talking to you."

- "Come when you're called — and say 'Coming' so I know you've heard me."

- "When someone asks you a question or says something to you, respond."[26]

When kids forget the rules, he says, remind them. Remember that rules help children learn self-discipline. "No television until homework's done," is not only reasonable, it teaches children temperance.

Here's a primer on establishing rules from the American College of Pediatricians' website, based on Laurence Steinberg's book *10 Basic Principles of Good Parenting*:

- All children need structure in their lives, and the best way to do this is to establish clear rules and limits.

- Be sure to establish rules that "make sense, that are appropriate to your child's age, and that are flexible enough to change as your child matures."

- Be firm in making your children keep the rules that have been appropriately set.[27]

Have Your "Teaching Toolbox" Ready

As Dr. Anderson points out, the word "discipline," which often has negative connotations, actually comes from the Greek word "to disciple." Think in advance about how you'll discipline, so that when the time comes you can reach into your figurative "toolbox." Dr. Anderson's preferred method of discipline for children is the time out, and she gives general guidelines for using it. Time out should be wherever the activity isn't. She recommends using a movable object, like a small chair or pillow, so it can be moved or taken elsewhere, such as to Grandma's house. At very young ages it should only be used for a few seconds. After time out, says Anderson, always give a hug and address the infraction by, for example, saying, "I love you, but you're not allowed to hit." You're telling the child you love him, but his behavior was inappropriate. "Time out provides the child with a nice, quiet, safe place where she can re-group, calm herself, get herself under control and think about her actions."[28] Dr. Trumbull believes that a playpen time out is reasonable at the age of fifteen months, and that most children are ready for a chair time out starting at eighteen months to two years.

For parents who use spanking as a method of discipline, there are parameters Dr. Trumbull recommends. Use it when milder measures have failed; it shouldn't be your first or only option. The typical ages for spanking are between two and six, because appealing to reason and consequences are less effective for smaller children. Spanking should always be a planned action; it should never be a reaction or made in anger. Spanking should never be harmful or cause bruising. To be specific, use an open hand to deliver one or two swats to the bottom. It should always occur in private, never in a public setting, in order to avoid humiliating the child. And it needs to be followed by a review of the offense, and the reassurance of the parents' unconditional love for the child.

It's important to note that the line between spanking and child abuse is hotly disputed these days. Legal challenges to parents spanking their children have been raised in several states, including New York, California, and Texas. In 2012, Delaware became the first state to ban parents from hitting their children, redefining child abuse as anything that causes "pain." Parents should be aware that they run the risk of being labeled child abusers if children complain to school teachers or administrators that they're spanked at home.

Here are some other age-appropriate disciplinary tools

and tips, courtesy of Dr. Trumbull:

- By age three and a half, privilege removal is a reasonable punishment.

- For school age children and teenagers, withdrawing privileges, grounding, and drawing fines out of allowances are appropriate and effective.

- Rewards can be useful teaching tools. For younger children, parents can reward good behavior with things such as stickers. For older children, rewards can take the form of increasing privileges.

In general, Trumbull says that parents need to remember that children also need affirmation and encouragement. Correction or punishment without affirmation will be counterproductive.

Assign Chores

Introduce household chores, like Kay Wills Wyma did. Her plan involved assigning a new chore every month to her five children. By the time a year was over, they not only cleaned their own rooms, they cleaned bathrooms, did laundry, and helped prepare meals. Wyma found that giving her children meaningful work fostered not only personal responsibility but emotional health, to say nothing of establishing parental authority. You don't need an elaborate plan, but you do need one that's age appropriate. Cleaning up toys is a good place to start. Then move up to making beds, putting dirty laundry in its place, setting and clearing the dinner table, helping with yard work, and cleaning bedrooms. The key — and often the hard part, as Wyma found out — is making sure the chores are completed and having a plan for what follows if they aren't. Be clear up front about the rewards and punishments.

Dr. Anderson believes chores are good for children in many ways. They don't just teach responsibility, they keep children — especially teenagers — connected to their families.

Establish Rituals

Simple rituals with kids, such as movie and game nights, or weekly visits to a library or coffee shop, can help forge and strengthen parent-child bonds.

Have Family Dinners

Family meals go a long way in cementing ties. In fact, there's research on the benefits of family dinners. The American College of Pediatricians examined a range of studies on the subject. They found evidence of so many advantages for families who had regular meals together that they now recommend their members encourage parents to partake of the family table. Better family relationships, healthier eating, better grades, and decreased drug and alcohol use by teens are just some of the many benefits of frequent (defined as five per week) family meals. "When families regularly share meals together," according to the ACPeds website, "everyone benefits — the children, parents and even the community."[29]

Shared meals can provide a sense of cohesion simply by bringing family members together. According to Drs. Jane Anderson and Den Trumbull, authors of the analysis, sitting down with each other at the end of the day allows families to reconnect, to communicate with one another, and to share values. Children like structure, and family meals help provide that. Dinnertime together is also a chance for children to observe how their parents interact and express emotions, and for the whole family to learn how to treat each other with respect. Teenagers who have more frequent meals with their families are more likely to report having positive relationships with them. Specifically, it doubles their chances of having "excellent relationships" with their fathers and with siblings.[30] According to one study, 71 percent of teens consider spending time with family members the best part of family meals.[31] Family dinners are an opportunity for kids to see their parents make family time a priority and for parents to share their values over the dinner table. Since this is time for kids to be with their families and not their peers, no cellphones allowed!

Take Family Vacations and Nurture Extended Family Relationships

Family vacations can also be valuable in strengthening family relations, and Dr. Sax believes they should be done without friends tagging along. Expensive trips to faraway places aren't necessary. Visit places such as historic sites and state and national parks and bring a picnic. In trying to connect your child to your culture and your values, it can help to live near extended family (if they share your values), so that other adults such as aunts, uncles, and grandparents can help offset peer influence. If that's not possible, there are other ways to have extended family members be part of your children's lives. Besides visiting them when possible, have your children use Skype and FaceTime to stay in touch and establish close relationships. Extended family members can become part of the authoritative community that children need, even from a distance.

Build a Community

Doherty writes about what author and fatherhood advocate James Levine and his wife did when their teenage daughter became a challenge. First, they arranged a meeting with the parents of their daughter's five closest friends. "Jim reports the result was an amazingly effective parent support group that met three times a year through their daughters' high school years. The group opened up channels of communication among the families, helped parents hold firm against sometimes unreasonable demands from their daughters, and helped their daughters resist unreasonable peer pressure." Don't go it alone! Seek out like-minded parents at church or at your children's school for support.

Expect Respect

Don't tolerate disrespect from your children. In *Take Back Your Kids*, Doherty advises parents to "challenge every disrespectful behavior — without exception — because that is the only way that the child will understand your expectations and the meaning of the behavior you want to extinguish." Maintain your own emotional control: be calm and focused. He recommends cultivating a tone of voice that communicates your seriousness.

It's never too late for parents who want to stop the disrespect they've allowed to go unchecked. Doherty advises encouraging children to become allies in changing things. "Children are happier when they are consistently respectful to the most important adults in their lives," he writes.[32]

Make a Family Mission Statement

Dr. Thomas Lickona recommends making a family mission statement. If you want to be clear about the values you want to foster in your children and the kind of behavior you expect from them, write out a mission statement that explicitly spells that out. He suggests posting it where everyone can see it and refer to it. Dr. Lickona provides this example of one family's mission statement:

- We commit to being kind, honest and trustworthy, and fair.

- We don't lie, cheat, steal, or hurt someone on purpose.

- We don't whine, complain, or make excuses.

- When we make a mistake, we make up for it, learn from it, and move on.

- We work to keep our minds, bodies, and souls healthy, strong, and pure.

- We commit to learning and growing in our faith through practice and trust in God's goodness.

- We live with an attitude of gratitude and joy.[33]

Have Family Meetings

This is another suggestion straight from Dr. Lickona, who believes that having regular family meetings is one of the best ways to build a positive family culture. Such meetings can also be used to solve problems, resolve sibling issues, and discuss policy on matters such as screen time and chores. "It's the time," he writes, "when you are the most explicit about the kind of family you want to be."[34] Dr. Lickona suggests starting with a half-hour meeting once a week and including popcorn or some kind of snack so it becomes something kids look forward to. Have one person speak at a time, with no interrupting, and focus on problem-solving instead of blame. It's an opportunity for parents to share their values and for children to participate in solving problems.

CHAPTER 2

SCHOOLS

When it comes to school, there are abundant opportunities for educators to encourage progressive attitudes and introduce concepts that are anathema to Christian parents. Much of this occurs in the context of sex education classes, which we will discuss in all its troubling detail in chapter four. Aside from those classes, schools are busily promoting the acceptance of gay lifestyles, so-called "same-sex marriage," and gender fluidity. These topics can easily be woven into regular classes without parental knowledge or consent.

Long before same-sex marriage was legal in any state and years before Caitlyn Jenner was gracing magazine covers, my children's school decided to put on an assembly for the elementary grades (kindergarten through fifth) called "Cootie Shots." Billed as an anti-bullying program, it was in fact a series of skits intended to introduce concepts like same-sex marriage and transgenderism. The sketch called "In Mommy's High Heels" speaks for itself. It was about a little boy who enjoyed dressing up like a girl.

That was bad enough. But the skit that we found most objectionable was called "The Duke Who Outlawed Jelly Beans." The story goes like this. After a young duke is temporarily put in charge of a kingdom, he first outlaws jelly beans. Next, he decrees that since he grew up with a mother and a father, that living arrangement will be the only one allowed. That puts at risk the boy who lives with his grandparents, the girl who lives only with her mother, and of course, the girl who lives with her two mommies. As my husband and I explained to the principal, the real message of the skit wasn't that people shouldn't be bullied — it was that all living arrangements are equal. A girl, for example, could easily take from it the message that when she has a child it won't matter whether there's a father in the picture. We cited the "Hardwired to Connect" study conducted by the YMCA of the USA, Dartmouth Medical School, and the Institute for American Values that recommended, among other things, that "we reevaluate our behavior and our dominant cultural values, and consider a range of changes in our laws and public policies, in order substantially to increase the proportion of U.S. children growing up with their two married parents."[35]

Our stepping forward and speaking up was to no avail. The assembly went on as planned. But here's the real kicker: The school did not intend for parents to know about the "Cootie Shots" assembly ahead of time. There was no announcement, no parental notification, no mention of it in any email blast. I happened to find out about it purely by accident and was able to inform a few like-minded friends. Thankfully we were able to have our kids skip it.

Given the fact that so-called "same-sex marriage" is now enshrined in law and that transgenderism is on a similar path to forced-acceptance, parents with children in private secular and public schools will be at a disadvantage. They'll likely have little control over whether those issues are discussed or how they're being presented. The fact is they may not even know if it's happening.

Excluding Parents
Examples abound of schools purposefully keeping parents out of the loop when it comes to controversial issues. In Emmaus, Pennsylvania, the student body at Emmaus High

School was shown a series of pro-LGBT videos.[35] Not only were parents not notified in advance, they weren't allowed to see the videos after the fact! In California, parents are up against the "Healthy Youth Act," passed in 2015, with two stated goals. As John Stonestreet writes at Breakpoint.org, the first is to "provide pupils with the knowledge and skills necessary to protect their sexual and reproductive health" from sexually transmitted diseases and unintended pregnancy. The second is "to give students 'knowledge and skills' to help them develop 'healthy attitudes' concerning 'body image, gender, sexual orientation, relationships, marriage and family.'"[36]

The law states that parents may "excuse their child from all or part of comprehensive sexual health education, HIV prevention education."[37] Here's the kicker: the law also states that parents are *not* allowed to excuse children from "instruction, materials, presentations, or programming that discuss gender, gender identity, gender expression, sexual orientation, discrimination ... relationships or family."[38] Many parents have missed that caveat, not realizing that they were *not* allowed to opt out of instruction related to gender ideology and sexual orientation. They made the mistaken assumption that they could opt out of all that's normally thought of as sex ed. As Stonestreet writes, "[P]arents in California can opt their kids out of the anatomy *but not the ideology*."[39]

No More Dick and Jane

Even for the youngest students, school libraries aren't what they used to be. By the time our children left elementary school, *King and King* was one of a couple books about homosexuality on the bookshelves. Aimed at children ages five to eight, according to Amazon, *King and King* tells the fictional story of a prince who marries a prince. My children could have stumbled across it on their own while visiting the library, or it could have been the librarian's choice to read aloud one day.

There are now plenty of children's books aimed at normalizing same-sex households. There's *Daddy, Papa and Me* and *Mommy, Mama and Me*, both for kids three years old and up. *King and King* now has a sequel — *King and King and Family* — in which the married kings adopt a little girl while on their honeymoon. You get the idea. It's quite likely such books are in your children's elementary school library. There's also nothing to stop a teacher from choosing such books for story time.

Let's take a moment to make one thing clear: Christianity is about loving God and loving one's neighbor. There is no place for bullying, mocking, or ridiculing others for any reason. That said, we are also obligated to live by God's rules. In the Catholic Church, and in traditional Protestant denominations, the rules about sex and marriage are straightforward: sex is intended exclusively for marriage, and marriage is the union of one man and one woman. There is a counter-moral message in those seemingly sweet books meant, in theory at least, simply to promote tolerance and respect. This morality is *not* in accord with basic Christian teaching. For traditional Christians, exposing young children to such books undermines both religious and parental authority.

The same can be said for the new crop of children's books on the topic of transgenderism. "Dyson loves pink, sparkly things. Sometimes he wears dresses," is part of the Amazon description of *My Princess Boy*, written for children ages four through eight. There's also *I Am Jazz*, the true story of Jazz Jennings who "from the time she was two years old ... knew that she had a girl's brain in a boy's body."[40] It's also intended for children starting at four years old. *Introducing Teddy*, for children ages three through six, is about a teddy bear named Thomas who reveals to his friend that he's really Tilly.

Much as LGBTQ activists and progressive educators would have us believe such books are aimed at helping children who are struggling with gender identity issues, for many parents — including Christians — it's more complicated than that. First there's the question of introducing the very idea to children. Dr. Michelle Cretella is a pediatrician, a Catholic mother of four, and president of the American College of Pediatricians. In an interview with me for *National Catholic Register*, she discussed the consequences of introducing the concept of transgenderism to young kids:

> Most parents with little children are going to be confronted by this at some point, whether it's in their public libraries, preschool or K-12 schools, just by virtue of the books that could be read to them. What is dangerous is that these young children are just developing the awareness of the fact that they are a boy or a girl. It's not until age seven that most realize that is who they are and that sex doesn't change. ... Children will come to believe that their sex is whatever they think they want it to be. This is dangerous from a psychological point of view. It's disrupting the natural process of gender identity formation.[41]

Dr. Cretella told me that it's important that both parents and children understand that it's our genes, our DNA, that determine our sex. Biological sex can't be changed; it's hardwired. Gender identity is what we feel and how we think about our biological sex. That, she says, is *not* hardwired. And around the age of seven, the idea of the permanence of biological sex is formed in a child's cognitive development.

Thus, reading children books that say people can be whatever sex and gender they choose is encouraging a lie. And if this is reinforced by parents and medical professionals who "affirm" a child's gender confusion, says Cretella, "the child will eventually be put on hormones that make him or her sterile, that harm bones, harm brain development, and increase the risk for stroke, diabetes and cancer over his lifetime."

There are critics who think the traditional Christian point of view is intolerant and unsympathetic. The truth is, we can have sympathy for people — children and adults — who suffer from gender dysphoria without tolerating educators teaching our children falsehoods.

Transgender Truths

Dr. Paul McHugh is the University Distinguished Service Professor of Psychiatry at Johns Hopkins Medical School and former psychiatrist in chief at Johns Hopkins Hospital. Writing for *The Public Discourse*, McHugh cites a thirty-year follow-up study of sex-reassigned individuals in Sweden where, he points out, the culture is "strongly supportive of the transgendered."[42] The study found evidence of "lifelong mental unrest," and suicide rates up to twenty times higher than for comparable peers. In other words, sex reassignment wasn't an answer. "The treatment should strive to correct the false, problematic nature of the assumption and to resolve the psychosocial conflicts provoking it. With youngsters, this is best done in family therapy," according to McHugh.

Walt Heyer has written extensively about transgenderism from a unique point of view: he used to be transgender. He agrees with McHugh that children who want to switch genders need intervention, not encouragement. Writing for *The Daily Signal*, Heyer says that by the age of four he wanted to be a girl.[43] He sought help from a gender specialist who told him the only way he'd find relief was by having gender reassignment surgery. And that's what he did at the age of forty-two, living as Laura Jensen for eight years. "While studying psychology in a university program, I discovered that trans kids most often are suffering from a variety of disorders, starting with depression — the result of personal loss, broken families, sexual abuse, and unstable homes," Heyer writes. "Deep depression leads kids to want to be someone other than who they are." This resonated with Heyer. "Finally, I had discovered the madness of the transgender life.

It is a fabrication born of mental disorders. I only wish that when I went to the gender counselor for help he would have told me I couldn't really change genders, that it is biologically impossible."

Gender Ideology in Schools

Parents at the Nova Classical Academy, a charter school in Minnesota, were confronted with the issue of transgenderism when the parents of a kindergarten boy insisted that he be treated as a girl by the school and his classmates. The school's existing anti-bullying program wasn't enough, they said. They wanted the issue addressed head on by, among other things, having the book *I Am Jazz* read in the kindergarten classroom. Some parents objected, and the student withdrew. His parents later sued the school for "allowing families to opt-out of classroom instruction on transgenderism, refusing to inform their son's classmates of his 'preferred' gender pronouns, and not allowing a pro-transgender book to be part of the kindergarteners' classroom instruction,"[44] according to a LifeSiteNews report. D.C. McAllister wrote about the case at *The Federalist*: "The child is a male who is confused about his gender. To play along with this psychological confusion instead of helping the child in a supportive and loving way to bring his thinking into alignment with reality is a form of child neglect, something no school should support."[45]

The parents of a six-year-old transgender girl successfully sued for discrimination when Eagleside Elementary school in Colorado wouldn't allow him/her to use the girls bathroom. It wasn't enough that they gave the child permission to use the restrooms in the teachers' lounge and the nurse's office. Similarly, the Nebraska School Activities Association now recognizes gender identity, rather than biological sex, as its standard for student athletes. The state's Catholic bishops expressed disappointment in the decision and said they would continue to urge that the policy be rescinded. This joint statement by the bishops is worth noting:

> Any person who experiences gender dysphoria is entitled to the respect that is the right of every human person, as well as genuine concern and the support needed for personal development and well-being. Such support, however, must be provided with due consideration to fairness; the safety, privacy, and rights of all students; and the truth about the human person.[46]

At Rocklin Academy charter schools near Sacramento, over forty families pulled their children out of the school as the board continued to defend a transgender lesson presented in kindergarten that included reading the book, *I Am Jazz*, by transgender activist Jazz Jennings.[47] Several parents said their five-year-olds were traumatized, and that they weren't notified beforehand. In Swampscott, Massachusetts, an elementary school principal announced that he was a woman and would now dress as a female. The Superintendent of Schools there has praised his "courage, honesty and transparency."[48] Teachers in the state of Maine are now forbidden to inform parents if their children identify as transgender while in school.[49]

Situations such as these will only increase as transgender rights take center stage in the culture. It will become increasingly difficult for parents not only to avoid having their children exposed to the idea of gender fluidity, but to avoid having it taught to them as gospel. Here's what Archbishop Paul Coakley of Oklahoma City wrote in a column for the archdiocesan website on this issue:

> Gender ideology is the next tsunami that threatens to sweep away centuries of accepted human wisdom about the complementarity and real differences between men and women. These differences are not merely about self-expression and personal choice. Sci-

ence, philosophy, theology and the accumulated wisdom of every culture have recognized that these differences are rooted in something real and objective. They are rooted in biology, and, more fundamentally, they are rooted in the design of the Creator.[50]

For parents who can afford it, many Catholic schools certainly offer a safer choice than public schools. But parents should still do their homework when choosing a school.

For example, Mercy High School in San Francisco, a Catholic girls college preparatory school, made the decision to allow a teacher who'd been at the school for four years to remain on staff, even as she "transitioned" to becoming a transgender man. Parents were sent a letter of explanation by the Sisters explaining that "we strive to witness to mercy when we honor the dignity of each person in a welcoming culture that pursues integrity of word and deed."[51] According to Daniel Guernsey of *Crisis Magazine*, the Sisters of Mercy also offered counseling "to help the students of the all-girls school accept the biologically female teacher's new gender identity as a man."[52]

Although the Sisters maintain they are being merciful to the teacher, by accepting her rejection of her biological sex they are assenting to what Pope Francis has called a false "gender ideology."[53] We could also question whether the decision is in the best interests of their students, which the sisters seem to at least tacitly acknowledge by their offer of counseling.

Daniel Guernsey is Director of K-12 Programs at the Cardinal Newman Society and writes that "the Vatican has taught for decades that Catholic school teachers are expected to uphold the Catholic faith in both word and deed." He quotes Canon Law, which states that "teachers are to be outstanding in correct doctrine and integrity of life" (Canon 802.2). Guernsey believes bishops and Catholic school leaders need to formalize policies and procedures for dealing with such situations.[54]

When speaking at the Shrine of Our Lady of Walsing-ham in Britain, Cardinal Raymond Burke addressed the difficulties facing Christian parents when it comes to education: "Today, parents must be especially vigilant, for sadly, in some places, schools have become the tools of a secular agenda inimical to the Christian life."[55]

Beyond Ideas

Schools normalizing ideas that run contrary to Catholic teaching is bad enough. But what about passing out condoms and emergency contraception? Think that's far-fetched? Here are some stories straight out of the headlines.

By the mid-1990s over 400 high schools in the United States had begun to distribute condoms by request to students. In 2014, a school district in Oregon decided to offer condoms to students from sixth grade on up, with no parental consent required.[56] Sixth graders are generally between eleven and twelve years old!

The Los Angeles Unified School District asked Planned Parenthood to run a health clinic at one of its high schools.[57] Students are allowed — *by law* — to visit the clinic without the permission of their parents. And the clinic is allowed to give students emergency contraception, birth control, pregnancy tests, and screening for sexually transmitted diseases. All the services are free and confidential. It's disconcerting to think that parents might get a call if their child requested an aspirin for a headache, but would have no clue if a nurse put her on birth control because she is sexually active.

Innocence Lost

In Massachusetts, thousands of students are asked to take The Massachusetts Youth Risk Behavior Survey every other year. Officially intended for high school students, the organization Mass Resistance claims that it's been administered as early as sixth grade in some cases.[58] Parents aren't even allowed to see the survey, and there's no "opt out" provision.[59]

As you'll see from the questions below taken from the 2015 survey, there are many ways to shatter innocence.

The first questions are innocuous enough: age, grade, ethnicity, average grades, height, weight, current living arrangements. Then come the kickers:

During the past 12 months, did you ever **seriously** *consider attempting suicide?*
  A. *Yes*
  B. *No*

During the past 12 months, did you **make a plan** *about how you would attempt suicide?*
  A. *Yes*
  B. *No*

During the last 12 months, how many times did you **actually attempt** *suicide?*
  A. *0 times*
  B. *1 time*
  C. *2 or 3 times*
  D. *4 or 5 times*
  E. *6 or more times*

Have you ever had sexual intercourse (oral, anal, vaginal)?
  A. *Yes*
  B. *No*

How old were you when you had sexual intercourse (oral, anal, vaginal) for the first time?
  A. *I have never had sexual intercourse*
  B. *11 years old or younger*
  C. *12 years old*
  D. *13 years old*
  E. *14 years old*
  F. *15 years old*

G. *16 years old*

H. *17 years old or older*

During your life, with how many people have you had sexual intercourse (oral, anal, vaginal)?

A. *I have never had sexual intercourse*

B. *1 person*

C. *2 people*

D. *3 people*

E. *4 people*

F. *5 people*

G. *6 or more people*

During the last 3 months, with how many people did you have sexual intercourse (oral, anal, vaginal)?

A. *I have never had sexual intercourse*

B. *I have had sexual intercourse, but not during the past 3 months*

C. *1 person*

D. *2 people*

E. *3 people*

F. *4 people*

G. *5 people*

H. *6 or more people*

The **last time** *you had sexual intercourse, what one method did you or your partner use to prevent pregnancy? (Select only one response.)*

A. *I have never had sexual intercourse*

B. *No method was used to prevent pregnancy*

C. *Plan B*

D. *Birth control pills*

E. *Condoms*

F. *An IUD (such as Mirena or ParaGard) or implant (such as Implanon or Nexplanon)*

G. *A shot (such as Depo-Provera), patch (such as Ortho*

Evra), or birth control ring (such as NuvaRing)
H. *Withdrawal or some other method*
I. *Not sure*

This isn't a survey I'd have wanted my kids to take at any age! The questions themselves are providing a kind of sex education which parents know nothing about. Imagine the discussions that must go on among students after these surveys, to say nothing of adding to the pressure kids already feel about keeping up with their peers when it comes to sex.

More than Music
Mass Resistance also reports that the Massachusetts Music Educators Association published an article advising school music teachers to provide "LGBTQ-friendly" classrooms.[60] Here are some of the steps they recommend:

- Change "heterosexual" lyrics in songs to be "queer" — and explain to students that not everyone is heterosexual.

- Use gender-neutral pronouns, such as "ze" instead of "he" or "she."

- Do not use terms such as "boys" and "girls" or have events where males and females dress or act differently.

- Share a list of LGBTQ-friendly resources, organizations, and websites with students. If possible, start a "gay-straight alliance" (GSA) club.

- Distribute material from the national LGBTQ organizations such as GLSEN. Become a proactive LGBTQ ally.

- Provide homosexual and transgender role models for students. (And come out to your students if you're L, G, B, T, or Q.)

- Display LGBTQ "safe space" stickers in the classroom.

Offensive Language Arts

At the Myron L. Powell School in Cedarville, New Jersey, eighth grade students were given an unusual homework assignment in Language Arts class.[61] They were to write a "reactive" response explaining what they would do in the following situation:

> You had a really rotten day, but lucky for you your best friend is having an awesome party later. You go to the party and start drinking. You have a little too much to drink and start talking to this girl/guy you've never seen before. You head upstairs to get better acquainted despite several friends telling you that you don't even know this person. You end up having sex with this person. The next day you really can't remember everything that happened and rely on your best friend to fill you in. A week later you find out that you contracted herpes from your one-night stand and that this is a disease that you will have all your life and never know when an outbreak will occur.

Speaking of English class, the Queer Straight Alliance at Acalanes High School in Lafayette, California, took over several ninth-grade English classes — with the school's approval — as part of a "tolerance workshop." According to Todd Starnes writing for Fox News, the students "were publicly shamed for disagreeing with speakers allowed to push an LGBT agenda."[62] The Pacific Justice Institute (PJI), which is representing parents upset about the incident, alleges that the students were instructed to stand in a circle where they were asked about their personal beliefs and their parents' beliefs about homosexuality. "The QSA had students step forward to demonstrate whether they believed that being gay was a choice and whether their parents would be accepting if they came out as gay," according to the PJI attorney. "Students who did not step forward were ridiculed and humiliated."[63] One parent told Starnes it was a public outing. "My child is being raised in a family with conservative values. We are a Christian family. What bothers me the most is the school is being dishonest and secretive about what's happening. My son's value system and our belief system is not being respected on many levels."[64]

Progressive ideas have dominated the education establishment for years. But it is only recently that educators have taken it upon themselves to attempt end-runs around parents by imposing beliefs on children that are contradictory to their family's values. This has made many schools a potential hazard when it comes to raising Catholic and other Christian kids.

I have read columnists who decry what they call "scaremongering" about what goes on in schools. My goal is not to frighten anyone, but rather to alert parents to the fact that they should not assume their values align with those taught at their local schools. I learned — sometimes too late — about the explicit and implicit lessons my children were being taught and which conflicted with my values.

Cardinal Raymond Burke had this to say on the subject of parents as primary educators of their children:

> Good parents and good citizens must be attentive to the curriculum which schools are following and to the life in the schools, in order to assure that our children are being formed in the human and Christian virtues and are not being deformed by indoc-

trination in the confusion and error concerning the most fundamental truths of human life and of the family, which will lead to their slavery to sin and, therefore, profound unhappiness, and to the destruction of culture.[65]

After all, the Church teaches that parents "have the first responsibility for the education of their children and they are the first heralds of the faith for them."[66]

SOLUTIONS, TIPS, & TOOLS

For Public Schools

The vast majority of Catholic and traditional Christian families use public schools to educate their children. A piece in *National Catholic Register* told the stories of three Catholic families who chose public schools and what they did to keep their children faithful. As the author put it, "Sending children to public school means that Catholic parents have to compensate for the religious education they aren't receiving each day in school."[67] The common thread among the parents was that they recognized the need to catechize their children themselves. One mother remembered their priest talking about how the family should serve as a domestic church, as the center of faith. "We have tried to do this through daily traditions: grace before meals, Advent and Lenten traditions, prayers before bedtime." She describes constantly talking about their faith and understanding the need to be intentional with it.

Another family made sure to reinforce what was being taught to their children in religious education classes, reading the Bible to them, and bringing faith into everyday conversations. Another chose to pray the Rosary as a family frequently. All of the families made a point of sending their kids to Catholic summer camps and took advantage of opportunities for them to attend World Youth Day and other events. One of the mothers took her younger children to daily Mass until they started middle school. As a family they participate in the March for Life every year.

One mother made the decision to pull her children out of sex education classes. Another reviewed in detail with the teachers what would be covered in sex ed and health classes and prepared her children ahead of time so they would understand the Church's teachings on those matters.

For parents who choose public schools, having an early, open, and frank discussion with school administrators about the importance of your faith may be helpful. If possible, do the same each year with your child's individual teachers. One of the families in the *Register* piece encountered some anti-Catholic bias in a history class. They met with the teacher and the head of the department, providing them a list of all the accomplishments of the Church throughout history. They explained that their daughter was being made to feel ashamed of her Catholic faith. Not only did the teacher apologize, he handed out copies of that list to every student in the class.

Parents who need help responding to LGBTQ activism in their child's school should visit truetolerance.org, run by Focus on the Family. It provides talking points, a list of "dos" and "don'ts" for approaching school officials, and practical advice. Do your homework by finding out what your school district's policies are when it comes to exempting children from controversial instruction. State laws vary regarding the opt-out rights of parents. The Family Policy Alliance, the public policy partner of Focus on the Family, provides resources to help parents understand state laws as they pertain to these issues. Try to find like-minded parents so that you can support each other should controversies arise.

Here is some advice from Focus on the Family for parents when meeting with school officials: "[W]e should be careful to conduct ourselves as ambassadors of Christ. ...

When you meet with the school administrators ... make a point of staying calm. Show respect and appeal to reason and logic. At the same time, stick to your guns and don't back down from your convictions."[68]

Parents may want to consider attending school board meetings, and even becoming involved in school board elections.

For Catholic and Other Christian Schools

Catholic and other Christian schools can be a great alternative to public education. In general, such schools have higher graduation and college acceptance rates than public schools. Parents, however, need to do their homework when considering a Catholic or Christian school, looking beyond test scores to the strength of the school's Christian culture and whether it accomplishes its faith mission.

Denise Donohue and Dan Guernsey are, respectively, the deputy director and director of the K-12 education programs at the Cardinal Newman Society. In a piece written for *National Catholic Register* they make some specific suggestions. Although their advice is aimed at Catholics, it can be applied to traditional Christians as well. They say that parents should look for "abundant evidence" that the faith informs all academic disciplines. They should find out whether the *Catechism of the Catholic Church* and Scripture are frequently referenced. And if sex education is taught, parents need to determine whether it's in line with Church teaching and "respectful of parents as the primary educators."[69]

Catholic schools should, they argue, reflect the warm atmosphere of family life, being both nurturing and supportive of students. Donohue and Guernsey suggest that parents see whether the school offers opportunities and requirements for charitable service. Other bellwethers to look for include whether the school offers frequent prayer, Mass, and Reconciliation.

On its website, the Cardinal Newman Society lists

schools with a strong Catholic identity in its Catholic Education Honor Roll. The Society has also issued a Parent Guide to help families ascertain the strengths and weaknesses of schools they're considering.[70]

Families may assume that tuition costs put Catholic schools out of reach for their children. The United States Conference of Catholic Bishops website has good information about a wide variety of financial assistance that may be available. Many schools offer scholarship programs, and some states provide tax relief and even education savings accounts that can help parents pay for a Catholic education for their children.[71]

For Homeschooling

Homeschooling is another choice more and more families, including Catholic and other Christian families, are making. According to the National Home Education Research Institute, as of 2016, 2.3 million children are homeschooled in the United States.[72] From a small movement that started in the 1980s largely among Christians, homeschooling has grown exponentially. Now legal in all fifty states, some allow homeschooled children to participate in public school sports. Some states also permit homeschooled students to take certain public school offerings, including Advanced Placement courses.

Parents who elect homeschooling have several options. There are home school curricula available that parents can use completely on their own. There are also some curricula that come with online support for both parents and students. Homeschooling families in many areas have formed cooperatives, with varying degrees of participation. Cooperatives function as support networks, with many offering homeschoolers the chance to play sports, play in an orchestra, or take field trips. Some have classes that meet regularly.

Another option is the homeschool/hybrid model, where children learn part-time at home with their parents and part-time in a formal classroom setting. Regina Caeli Academy is one such program offering, according to its website, a "classical hybrid education in the Catholic tradition."[73]

The Home School Legal Defense Association was formed to protect the legal rights of homeschooling families. Additionally, the HSLDA website has links to support groups, information for parents considering homeschooling, and information on how to get started.[74]

The Home School Foundation is the charitable arm of the HSLDA and helps provide financial and other support for homeschooling families. Its website provides a list of more affordable home school curricula, in addition to links to help parents find local homeschooling groups.

Writing on the EWTN website, Mary Kay Clark has this advice for parents considering the homeschooling option:

> Once you have decided to teach your own children, you should decide whether to teach from your own lessons or to enroll your children in one of the Catholic correspondence schools, such as Seton Home Study School. ... An important first step is to write out a Statement of Philosophy, to make it clear to yourself, your spouse, and your children what you hope to accomplish. Why is a Home School necessary? What are your purposes? What are the values you intend to impart to your children? Your Statement of Philosophy should be in positive terms however, and not simply reflect your objections to something in the local schools. It is vital that you and your spouse agree on the Statement and, if you enroll in a Home Study School, their Statement of Philosophy should agree with yours."[75]

CHAPTER 3
MEDIA

There's no question that digital media has become a dominant force — if not *the* dominant force — in the lives of young people. Its influence (and potential influence) cannot be underestimated. This chapter is about all forms of media (defined as anything that allows for mass communication), with a special emphasis on digital and social media. For that reason, this chapter will cover the following:

- Digital media (accessed via digital devices such as laptops, tablets, and smartphones), comprised of social media sites (e.g., YouTube, Instagram, Snapchat, Facebook), streaming videos, online video games, websites, etc., and

- Traditional forms of media such as television, movies, magazines, and books.

According to statistics compiled by the American College of Pediatricians, the average child spends about seven and a half hours a day using media.[76] On a typical day, eight to eighteen-year-olds spend about four and a half hours watching television, one and a half hours using computers, and less time on other media such as video games, books, magazines, and movies. Some studies put the figure even higher for older children and teens. It has become the leading activity for children and teens other than sleeping. That's a lot of time, a lot of content, and a huge opportunity for the world to exert its influence over young minds.

According to the Pew Research Center, 89 percent of teens use social media. And as of 2018, 95 percent of teens either have or have access to smartphones. A Kaiser Family Foundation study found that only 28 percent of children and teens report having rules and restrictions from their parents about the amount of time spent with media in general.[77]

Research conducted by Common Sense Media in 2017 found that 42 percent of children ages one to eight have their own tablet device. The average amount of time spent with media devices in that age group increased from five minutes a day in 2011 to forty-eight minutes a day in 2017. About one in ten children under the age of eight has a "smart" toy that connects to the internet, or a voice-activated assistant device available to them at home.[78]

Digital media in particular is playing an overwhelming role in the lives of children and adolescents. Excessive and developmentally inappropriate use carries what the American College of Pediatricians call "grave health risks for children and families."[79] Besides higher risks of obesity, lower academic performance, and sleep problems, there are increased risks for depression and high-risk behaviors, including sexual activity at an earlier age. Even the more progressive American Academy of Pediatrics includes this in its policy statement on media:

> The overwhelming penetration of media into children's and teenagers' lives necessitates a renewed commitment to changing the way pediatricians, parents, teachers, and society address the use of media to mitigate potential health risks and foster appropriate media use.[80]

There are risks associated with the use of media that can interfere with your efforts to keep your kids spiritually and emotionally healthy. It seems obvious that parents trying to raise faithful, virtuous, principled kids need to manage the media they consume.

A Matter of (Screen) Time

Like the Kaiser Family Foundation, the American College of Pediatricians reports that the majority of children live in homes where parents make no rules regarding the amount of time spent in front of screens. As the ACPeds position paper on media use puts it, "Time spent with 'screen use' must be taken from other more potentially beneficial activities of the day — personal 'face-to-face' communication and interaction with family and friends, outdoor play (with its associated benefits of creativity, problem solving, and exercise), reading, homework, doing chores, and sleeping."[81] Aside from the question of what messages children and adolescents are getting from their screens, there is the matter of influence. We've discussed how important it is for parents to be the primary influence in their children's lives. More time spent in front of screens and with traditional media means less time with parents and other family members. In the battle for influence, time counts.

There is also growing evidence that spending time in front of screens in and of itself may be detrimental to a child's psychological and emotional well-being. Jean Twenge is a psychologist and the author of the 2017 book, *iGen: Why Today's Super-Connected Kids Are Growing Up Less Rebellious, More Tolerant, Less Happy — and Completely Unprepared for Adulthood — and What That Means for the Rest of Us.* In a piece for *The Conversation* in 2018, Twenge writes about newer research she conducted with Keith Campbell. They found that children and teens who spent more time using screens scored lower in eighteen of nineteen indicators of well-being. "After one hour a day of use, children and teens who spent more time on screens were lower in psychological well-being: They were less curious and more easily distracted, and had a more difficult time making friends, managing their anger and finishing tasks. Teens who spent an excessive amount of time on screens were twice as likely to have been diagnosed with anxiety or depression." She notes that the research is not correlational. In other words, it's not clear whether the screen time leads to depression and anxiety, or whether kids who are depressed or anxious are more likely to spend more time in front of screens. "Either way," she writes, "excessive screen time is a potential red flag for anxiety, depression and attention issues among children and teens."[82]

Television and Streaming Services

According to figures from the A.C. Nielsen Company, 99 percent of U.S. households have at least one television. Most, in fact, have more than one, and many of those are in children's bedrooms. The Parents Television Council reports that two-thirds of all children in the United States have televisions in their bedroom. Thanks to virtually countless cable offerings, and streaming services such as Netflix, Hulu, and Amazon Prime, viewers today can take their pick of everything from fine art to pure raunch. Not to mention that there are commercials for everything from erectile dysfunction remedies to products once euphemistically referred to as marital aids. It all adds up to a huge challenge for parents trying to protect their children from seeing inappropriate content.

Another problem for parents is that television viewing isn't just on televisions any more. *Adweek* predicts that within a few years "mobile devices will overtake TVs as the primary way consumers watch their favorite shows." So overseeing TV viewing for children is more complicated than it used to be. And although there's plenty of good content on television for children, there's plenty that isn't.

Let's talk about violence. The University of Michigan

details studies that point to two headlines for parents: there's a lot of violence on television (including in programs for children) and watching violence can affect children's behavior.[83] It's estimated that an average American child will see 200,000 violent acts and 16,000 murders on TV by the time they're eighteen years old. Most violent acts in movies and television shows go unpunished and are often portrayed as humorous. Many shows glamorize violence. Consider this: "Repeated exposure to TV violence makes children less sensitive toward its effects on victims and the human suffering it causes."[84] So if we want to raise empathic, caring human beings, we must be aware of violence on television. This includes deciding which programs are appropriate and which are not, and sticking to those rules.

Then there's sex. There's no question that sex is a very real presence on TV. From prime-time dramas to daytime talk shows, it's hard to miss discussions or portrayals of sex. Here's what the University of Michigan found on the subject.

> Kids are probably not learning what their parents would like them to learn about sex from TV ... seventy percent of the top twenty most-watched shows by teens include sexual content. Fifteen percent of scenes with sexual intercourse depict characters that have just met having sex. ... Watching sex on TV increases the chances a teen will have sex and may cause teens to start having sex at younger ages. Even viewing shows with characters talking about sex increases the likelihood of sexual initiation.[85]

Here's some more evidence from the American College of Pediatricians: "Studies reveal that the more an adolescent watches television programming featuring sexual content, the more likely that adolescent is to prematurely initiate sexual activity. ... These studies also documented that teens who were exposed to *talk* about sex on television experienced risks similar to those teens who *viewed* actual sexual behavior."[86] If we want our children to understand sex in the context of Christianity, we can't let the culture do the teaching. It should be noted that, though the University of Michigan study is the most complete one currently available, it was conducted in 2010. Considering that television content now extends beyond network and cable offerings to streaming services, it's reasonable to assume children are now subject to even wider exposure to sex and violence.

TV shows with themes that normalize homosexuality and same-sex marriage are also problematic for Christian families. *Will and Grace* (both the original and the reboot), *Modern Family*, and *Glee* became mainstream prime-time network hits. The Disney Channel recently made history of sorts with a show aimed at tweens called *Andi Mack*. It includes a story line about a young character's "journey to self-acceptance as a gay person." An episode of the Disney Junior show *Doc McStuffins*, aimed at preschoolers, featured a family with two moms. Sadly, it's likely just the start of things to come.

In its "Parent's Guide to Streaming Video," the Parent Television Council warns parents about the hazards of streaming services when it comes to children. Some of their major findings include the fact that among the top SVOD (Streaming Video On Demand) providers, "there is no consistency in the application or visibility of aged-based content ratings." Netflix offers pornographic content whose titles often appear near child-friendly categories. Similarly, Amazon Prime has adult-themed titles that children might have to scroll past. None of the SVOD services offer parents the option to block all explicit titles at all times across all devices. Just as one example of the ever-increasing original programming by streaming services, Netflix made headlines with its original production of a series aimed at young people, *13 Reasons Why*, about the reasons behind a teen's suicide. Calling it intense and dark, Common Sense Media reports that the show includes a graphic rape scene, and that the suicide is "shown in great detail."

Commercials can be potential landmines for families watching television, too. A show suitable for children may contain commercials that aren't. This could include such things as a promo for another show airing later in the evening, a trailer for an R-rated movie, or a Victoria's Secret ad.

Cellphones and Other Screens

Cellphones, especially smartphones, are for most teenagers and tweens the way they communicate with each other and with the world. Whether it's texting on a non-internet connected cellphone, or using YouTube, Instagram, Snapchat, and Facebook on a smartphone, it's how young people stay connected. A 2018 Pew Research Center study found that 95 percent of teenagers had access to smartphones, with 45 percent saying they're online "almost constantly."[87] Many of the negative influences the world has to offer — pornography, sexting, overuse of social media, online bullying, and peer pressure — reach kids through their phones. Statistics cited by the Marriage and Religion Research Institute indicate that 75 percent of porn-watching is done on smartphones. And 25 percent of *all* internet searches are for pornography. Yet, the potential dangers of cellphones go beyond the obvious ones of accessing harmful and inappropriate material.

In her book, *Be the Parent, Please: Stop Banning Seesaws and Start Banning Snapchat*, author Naomi Schaefer Riley writes about how phones can impact children. She quotes clinical psychologist Mark Lerner who believes many of the mental health issues facing young people can be traced to technology. Being in constant touch with what's going on in the world or with peers can be harmful. "These mechanisms of distribution are overwhelming us with information," Lerner says. He recalls being out on a fishing boat with his son who, after checking his iPhone, reported that Robin Williams had just committed suicide. With cellphones by our sides, it's difficult to get away from the world, difficult not to be distracted, difficult to distinguish between what truly matters and what doesn't. Here's how Riley sums up the dangers of cellphones for children:

> It is not an exaggeration to say that giving your kids a cellphone is giving them the keys to the kingdom. There is a whole world out there that they can now access without your knowledge. That world, which will be constantly beeping at your child, will forever change him or her. It may change how your child views friendships, how he or she interacts with the outdoors, how he or she experiences time alone. When we hand over phones and tablets to children, we are likely to be changing not only the information they can access but also their habits, their personalities, and their tastes.[88]

In her book, psychologist Jean Twenge writes about members of what she calls iGen — those born between 1995 and 2012 — who have grown up with smartphones and don't remember a time before the internet. In a piece for *The Atlantic*, Twenge writes that there is "compelling evidence that the devices we've placed in young people's hands are having profound effects on their lives — and making them seriously unhappy."[89] She cites a survey called Monitoring the Future, funded by the National Institute on Drug Abuse, which has been surveying teenagers over a period of several years. Among other things, kids are asked about their happiness levels, their social interactions, their social media use, and their onscreen time. The results, she says, are clear. Teens who spend more time on screens are more likely to be unhappy, and vice versa. Twenge reports that studies have found a correlation between time spent online and mental health problems, specifically depression. Suicide risk factors for teens rose significantly when they spent two or more hours a day online.

Even though there are filters available for digital devices that can help protect against accessing inappropriate material, smartphones and tablets allow kids to download apps. There are plenty of apps you wouldn't want your child to have. "Amino" apps, also called affinity-based apps, are for people with shared interests. They allow kids and teens to find a host of others who enjoy the same things they do such as stamp collecting or playing obscure musical instruments. As John Stonestreet writes at Breakpoint, it all sounds harmless enough until you realize where those apps can lead children. "Recently, after speaking at a conference," Stonestreet reports, "a father came up to me crying, telling me that in just three clicks of his ten-year-old daughter's Amino account, he found unmoderated discussions of sexual identity, pansexuality, bulimia, anorexia and suicide."[90] Stonestreet draws parents' attention to a specific affinity-based app called Musical. ly. Designed as a lip-syncing app, users can upload videos of themselves. In researching the site, however, writer Anastasia Basil instead found "a world of cyberbullying, kids chatting about self-harm, and streaming homemade pornography. There were children calling themselves ugly, uploading videos about suicide methods, and promoting eating disorders." Besides the fact that these apps are unmonitored, and no one is accountable for the content, there are also predators who use them as a means of identifying potential targets.

Many apps allow for instant live streaming of daily activities. Examples include Meerkat, Periscope, YouNow, and Twitch. The American College of Pediatricians reports that "many teens are broadcasting from their bedrooms, including leaving their cellphones on to broadcast while they are sleeping."[91]

Social Media
Many teens, but especially girls, live their lives out on social media sites such as Instagram, Snapchat, and Facebook —

or, at least, they portray the lives they want their peers to see. That's the trouble. For many, sharing on social media isn't about expressing who they really are, it's about creating a persona. In his book, *Girls on The Edge*, pediatrician and psychologist Leonard Sax talks about the potential dangers of social media sites. As one seventeen-year-old told him regarding Facebook, "It's not about being authentic. It's about being cool."[92] There's a kind of hyper-connectedness and a need to track what everyone else is doing, which leaves tweens and teens little time to reflect on who they really are, or who they want to become. It also increases the influence of peers over parents.

In her piece for *The Atlantic*, psychologist Jean Twenge points out another downside of being hyper-connected. "For all their power to link kids day and night, social media also exacerbates the age-old teen concern about being left out."[93] Thanks to sites such as Instagram and Facebook, teens know — often in real time — what their friends (or "friends") are doing. "Those not invited to come along are keenly aware of it. Accordingly, the number of teens who feel left out has reached all-time highs across age groups," Twenge writes. "Like the increase in loneliness, the upswing in feeling left out has been swift and significant."

The pressure to be liked, or to "get likes," on social media is enormous, especially for girls, according to Twenge. One of the teenage girls she interviewed for her research described feeling nervous about what people would think and say about her posts on Instagram. Twenge calls it a "psychic tax" that's levied on teens as they wait for affirmation in the form of positive comments and "likes." Social media ramps up the peer pressure most teenagers already feel to fit in with the crowd. That can make life especially difficult for Christian teens attempting to live out their faith.

Then there are the negative comments, the hurtful rumors, and mean messages designed to ostracize and exclude other teens, which have come to be known as cyberbullying. According to Twenge and the Cyberbullying Research Center, girls are more likely to be the victims of such online assaults, which can be very damaging emotionally and psychologically. A 2018 Pew Research Center survey found that 59 percent of teens have experienced some form of cyberbullying.[94]

According to TeenSafe, Snapchat is the fastest growing social media app at the moment, with four out of ten teens making use of it.[95] It has an estimated eighty-two million users, most of them between the ages of thirteen and twenty-five. Here's how it works: users can send photos or videos along with text messages which then disappear from the receiver's phone within a few seconds after being viewed. As TeenSafe puts it, "The app has become a hotbed for sexting and cyberbullying among all ages, in part thanks to how it operates." It's popular because the content is (in theory) viewed only by the recipient, and not by Facebook "friends" or Instagram "followers." However, both the sender and recipient can take a screenshot of the message and send it on to others. It's also anonymous, making it especially attractive to those who want to engage in sexting and cyberbullying. TeenSafe reports that the FBI has warned that pedophiles are using Snapchat to solicit photos from young teenagers.

Snapchat also has a feature called Discover,[96] which is troublesome. Here's how it works according to TeenSafe: "When in the Snapchat app, a subscriber can click on Discover and see channels from content publishers with high ranking Snapchat channels. The problem is that many of these high ranking channels offer sexually oriented content." So the dangers of Snapchat go beyond what a child might send or receive, to what they might be exposed to in Discover.

Another phenomenon of living in a cyber world is what columnist Clive Thompson calls the "microcelebrity." Teenage girls getting ready for a party "make sure they're dressed for their close-up," he wrote for *Wired* magazine, "because they know there *will* be photos and those photos *will* end up online."[97] The danger, says Sax, is that teens who get caught up in what he calls the "cyberbubble" will find it hard "to know where they came from, where they are, and where they want to go."[98] Overly concerned about the image they present to the world, they won't feel at home with who they are. We want our children to know who they are and where they belong in God's scheme of things. We can't let them become people they think the world wants them to be.

Girls on The Edge is not written from a Christian worldview. However, Sax raises the issue of "an unsatisfied appetite for the spiritual" and its effect on young women. No doubt the same applies to young men. Sax quotes Courtney Martin, a young author who's written about her own struggles and those of her friends. "Some of us, for lack of a 'capital G' God, have searched out little gods. We worship technology, celebrities, basketball players, rock stars, supermodels, [and] video games. These empty substitute rituals, this misguided worship, intellectualization, addiction to moving fast has led my generation to a dark and lonely place."[99] Citing various studies, Sax notes that adolescent girls who are involved in their religious communities are less likely to smoke, drink alcohol, use marijuana, and be preoccupied with physical appearance. They're also considerably less likely to suffer from depression. "If girls are not healthy spiritually they may find themselves not so much *living* as *performing*."[100] The definition of peer pressure is that kids feel the need to "fit in" with their social group and adjust their behavior accordingly. Social media sites and constant connections with peers via texting magnifies the potential influence of peer pressure. Young people, both male and female, may think they're living their own authentic lives when they are, in fact, merely putting on a show for their peers.

As already noted, some studies have found that spending more time specifically on social media (as opposed to being online for other reasons) leads to more unhappiness among teenagers. Though sites such as Instagram and Facebook are supposed to connect people to "friends," psychologist Jean Twenge writes that teens who use social media are actually more lonely than previous generations: "[W]hen teens spend more time on smartphones and less time on in-person social interactions, loneliness is more common. So is depression."[101]

Sexting

A discussion of social media wouldn't be complete without noting the phenomenon of what's known as "sexting." In her book *American Girls: Social Media and the Secret Lives of Teenagers*, Nancy Jo Sales reports on the interviews she conducted with 200 teenagers and talks about the intense pressure they feel to send and receive sexually suggestive and even explicit photos on their cellphones. "It's safe to say that sexting is part of the culture of social media; whether or not a girl is sexting, she's most likely aware of the practice."[102] In fact, a 2018 study published in *JAMA Pediatrics* found that almost 15 percent of teens had sent a sext, while about 27 percent had received one.[103] For the record, here's the definition of sexting, as given by one of the study's co-authors: "The sharing of sexually explicit images and videos of oneself through the internet or electronic devices, such as smartphones." As parents, we must be aware that this is a serious phenomenon. Your child could find him or herself under pressure to go along with the crowd. It may seem obvious that sexting is simply wrong and contrary to Christian morality, but it may not be obvious to your children. In addition, there are potentially devastating legal ramifications if kids are caught sexting: they could be charged with the production, distribution, or possession of child pornography.

Another related phenomenon is non-consensual sexting among teens, i.e., when one person forwards a sext without permission. In the *JAMA Pediatrics* study, researchers reported that 12 percent of teens have forwarded a sext without permission, and 8.4 percent have had their photo forwarded without consent.[104] Beyond the obvious issues of embarrassment, teens can become victims of harassment, cyberbullying, and even blackmail.

At LifeSiteNews, Jonathan Van Maren writes about his travels and talks at high schools across the country related to the prevalence of pornography and sexting among teenagers. "One teen told me that the pressure to send [nude] pictures was 'relentless,' and that the guys simply didn't stop asking until the girls caved and sent one."[105] He reports that sexting is prevalent, including at Christian schools. "I would go so far as to say that it is common in Christian schools, and that one of the reasons this practice has spread so far and so fast is that parents are not even aware that this is taking place — even though their children are making horrifyingly permanent decisions that will impact the rest of their lives."

Other Forms of Popular Entertainment

Like television, other forms of popular entertainment are much more likely to reflect modern culture than a Christian worldview. Parents need to know that there are seriously problematic ideas found in books, movies, music, and video games aimed at young people.

I remember when the *Gossip Girl* series became popular and my then-twelve-year-old daughter wanted to read what "all" her friends were reading. I headed to the "young adult" section at my local big-chain bookstore and spotted *Gossip Girl* and its sequels alongside the more well-known and reliably wholesome *Anne of Green Gables* and *Princess Diaries* series. Posted on the shelves were several notices that read: "Some Young Adult titles contain mature content. Parental supervision is recommended." It was certainly enough to give a parent pause, so I dutifully dove into the first book of the series to see whether it was suitable for a twelve-year-old. It didn't take me long. By the second paragraph in, the main character, a high school girl, is swilling back scotch, upset because she doesn't like her mother's new boyfriend. The second chapter is titled "An Hour of Sex Burns 360 Calories." If a movie contained the foul language this book does, it would be rated "R." The blurb from *Teen People* magazine said it all, describing the book as "Sex and the City for the younger set." Therefore, though we may be happy to see our kids reading instead of watching TV, *what* they're reading matters. Many books today that are considered appropriate for tweens and teens can easily corrupt young minds and work against the values Christian parents are trying to instill. It should be noted that the Gossip Girl books spawned a wildly popular TV series — as inappropriate as the books — that's available for streaming on sites like Netflix.

In its position paper, "The Impact of Media Use and Screen Time on Children, Adolescents, and Families," the American College of Pediatricians expresses concern over video games. The ACPeds website notes that parents of toddlers are increasingly using games on their smartphones to entertain their young children. "Children and adolescents who spend time playing video games (especially violent games) are more likely to have difficulties paying attention in school; act aggressively toward others; interpret others' behaviors more negatively; have decreased empathy; have less pro-social behavior; and respond more violently when confronted."[106] The most popular video games are the most violent, and parents typically provide less oversight over them than they do for television. According to the ACPeds, 90 percent of teens in grades eight through twelve reported that their parents don't check the ratings of the video games they purchase, and 89 percent say their parents don't put limits on the time they're allowed to play them.

Similar to other forms of popular culture, video games present two potential problems: content that may be counter to Christian values and outsized influence if too much time is spent playing them.

Movies come with ratings that might not align with your opinions about what is age appropriate for your children. As with television, early exposure to sexual content in popular mainstream movies correlates with an earlier age of sexual debut and engagement in risky sexual behaviors. In other words, abstinence till marriage is going to be a tough sell for kids who've absorbed society's casual attitudes about sex through movies and other media.

To say that teen magazines aren't what they used to be is a gross understatement. In its July 2017 issue, *Teen Vogue* published a story called "Anal Sex: What You Need to Know." The tagline of the article reads, "How to do it the RIGHT way."[107] "There is no wrong way to experience sexuality, and no way is better than any other," the author wrote. Describing the act as "perfectly normal," she went on to say that it "can be awesome, and if you want to give it a go, you do that. More power to you." I'll spare you the explicit details, but the bottom line is that the magazine was encouraging and instructing teenagers regarding how to engage in sodomy. An issue published soon after that included a piece called "Back to School Awards 2017: The Best Health and Wellness Products."[108] Its recommended items included "personal massagers," lubricants, and condoms.

All the Noise

Technology has made the world a noisier place for most of us, including our children. Our lives are filled with the clamor of the world's distractions. "The world is too much with us," are words written by the poet William Wordsworth over two centuries ago. Perhaps those words have always been true. But today our cellphones buzz, our tablets chirp, and our televisions blare incessantly with news, gossip, or entertainment. The world intrudes relentlessly in ways that didn't exist only a generation ago. Peace of mind can be hard to come by when there is no quiet time and no opportunity for solitude.

In his book, *The Power of Silence: Against the Dictatorship of Noise*, Cardinal Robert Sarah talks about the importance of silence when it comes to knowing God. "Nothing will make us discover God better than his silence inscribed in the center of our being," he writes. "If we do not cultivate this silence, how can we find God?"[109] He goes on to quote a homily given by Benedict XVI in which the then-Pope said that "we live in a society in which it seems that every space, every moment must be 'filled' with projects, activities and noise; there is often no time even to listen or to converse. Dear brothers and sisters, let us not fear to create silence, within and outside ourselves, if we wish to be able not only to become aware of God's voice but also to make out the voice of the person beside us, the voices of others."[110]

We and our children are immersed in a noisy, media-filled world that can be hard to escape. But if we want our children to have a relationship with God, we must find ways of setting the world aside and cultivating silence. "In silence, not in the turmoil and noise," Cardinal Sarah writes, "God enters into the innermost depths of our being."[111]

SOLUTIONS, TIPS, & TOOLS

For Television and Streaming Services

Know the Shows

The Parents Television Council was started in 1995 to help families protect children from inappropriate content. Its website, www.parentstv.org, offers viewing guides, reviews, program suggestions, and advice on exactly what kinds of safeguards are available for both regular TV viewing and streaming services. Parents can get detailed information about specific programs from the PTC website. It offers a "Family Guide® to Prime Time Television," complete with its own ratings for programs, which may differ considerably from industry ratings. There are "Picks of the Week" suggestions for family-friendly viewing, along with information on sorting out fact from fiction when it comes to how media can affect children. Detailed information for parents on streaming services is also available on the PTC website. "Over-the-Top or a Race to the Bottom: A Parent's Guide to Streaming Video" includes rankings for streaming services, and also spells out the pros and cons of OTT devices such as Chromecast, AppleTV, and AmazonFireTV.

Common Sense Media is chock full of valuable information for parents when it comes to navigating both media and technology. CSM offers parent-geared reviews for TV shows, including those on streaming sites.[112]

PluggedIn.com is another great resource for parents. Run by Focus on the Family, the PluggedIn website reports on all forms of popular culture, including television. It offers detailed descriptions of shows, including those on streaming services, pointing out content that is sexual, violent, or relates to drugs and alcohol. Its reviews cover language and general themes, including spiritual ones.

Check the Channels

Look for channels that can be trusted to have appropriate content — even during commercials — such as the Hallmark Channel, Up TV, and INSP TV. For younger children, Nick Jr. TV and Disney Junior don't rely as much on advertisements as their counterparts for older children. Public television has commercial-free educational programs, including documentaries and classical music concerts. Streaming services such as Amazon Prime, YouTube, and Netflix offer children's programming with the advantage of being commercial-free and available at the customer's convenience.

Though there is always the option of having a TV-free home, for many families that's not a viable choice. The problem isn't the television itself. As Rebecca Hagelin writes in her book, *30 Ways in 30 Days to Save Your Family*, "the problem is lack of parental oversight."[113]

Watch Together

Whenever possible, watch with your children. You'll know

what programs they're seeing and what lessons they're receiving. Doing so allows for "teachable moments" regarding both content and commercials.

Explain Commercials
When your children watch commercial programming, be sure to explain ahead of time what commercials are. Children can and should understand that commercials are designed to encourage us to spend money, and that we don't need certain products in order to be happy.

Limit TV Time
Limit the amount of time kids spend watching TV, whether it's on television sets or on mobile devices. The American Academy of Pediatrics recommends *no* screen time for children under the age of three. From age three to seven, they suggest no more than twenty to thirty minutes a day.

Record Ahead of Time
Using a Digital Video Recorder (DVR) or TIVO allows parents to record programs and skip the commercials. It also allows them to preview programs in advance. Many cable companies offer DVRs as part of their service.

Use Blocking Technology and Parental Controls
Cable companies typically offer set top boxes that allow customers to block individual titles, entire networks, or programs based on ratings. In addition, if you have a television made after the year 2000, it has a V-chip installed. Like set top boxes, parents can use the V-chip to block programming based on show ratings. Be aware that mature content is often not accurately labeled, and there is no descriptor for violent content. Also, parents may have different views about what constitutes a PG or TV-14 rating and should either preview the program or check the PTC website for details on content.

Some streaming services offer the option of using parental controls. Netflix allows parents to set a PIN for specific maturity ratings and/or for a specific television series or movie. Parents who use Amazon Prime can block the playback of videos based on ratings categories. In addition, Amazon Fire TV devices have their own parental control settings to block access to content based on ratings. YouTube's parental controls are called Safety Mode. Once activated on computers and/or mobile devices, the site uses age-restriction settings and other means of filtering videos unsuitable for children. For Hulu, parents can set up a child's profile which limits their access to the Hulu Kids library.

Know What's Being Downloaded

Keep in mind that many television shows can be downloaded onto computers and smartphones. The American College of Pediatricians cites data indicating that approximately 40 percent of "television" viewing by adolescents takes place on other devices. *Business Insider* reports on the popularity of streaming services over live TV among teens, who watch twice as much Netflix compared to regular television.[114] Most of that viewing is being done on smartphones, according to a study by AwesomenessTV.[115] So make sure your teenagers know what shows they can and cannot watch, and monitor their downloads to be sure they're listening. If your teens have smartphones, be sure to make use of the parental controls discussed above to supervise and limit their video streaming capabilities.

For cellphones and other screens

Be in Charge

Chances are you're footing the bill for the cellphones/smartphones, tablets, and computers your kids have. From the very beginning, insist on knowing passwords and logins, and reserve the right to monitor their devices. Even if kids protest, they may actually feel safer knowing you're looking over their shoulders. Make it clear that having a phone is a privilege, not a right.

For author Leonard Sax, the issue is protection, and he believes parents should oversee their children's computers and cellphones. Children should know parents are watching their online activities and the reasons such monitoring is necessary. He specifically recommends a service called Net Nanny (netnanny.com), which allows parents to track every site their children visit and also lets parents limit the amount of time spent online.

The American College of Pediatricians cites two interesting statistics on the issue of parental oversight. First, though 90 percent of teens say their parents trust them to be responsible online, 45 percent say they would change something about their online behavior if their parents were watching. Second, almost 70 percent of pre-teens admit to hiding online activities.[116]

Use "Dumb" Phones

Wait as long as possible before giving your children phones and start with "dumb" phones that don't connect to the internet. Author Naomi Schaefer Riley recommends waiting until at least high school before allowing kids to use smartphones.

In a piece called "Parents' Dilemma: When to Give the Children Smartphones," *The Wall Street Journal* included the story of one mother in California. Felice Ahn, a mother of two preteen daughters in Palo Alto, made the decision not to give them smartphones even when they reach high school. She and her husband (who works for a major tech company) are concerned that the devices could impede the girls' development and create negative social pressures. "Maybe the pendulum will begin to swing," Ahn told the *WSJ*. "Maybe this approach won't be so much like a fish swimming upstream."[117] For now the family has decided to take a different approach because, as Ahn puts it, smartphones "bring the outside in. We want the family to be the center of gravity."

Limit Use

Don't allow phones at the dinner table and keep them out of children's bedrooms, especially at night. Author Naomi Schaefer Riley describes how one mother with two preteen daughters handled the phone issue in her household. When her daughters reached middle school, each of them got a "dumb" phone to be in touch with her about school drop-offs and pickups, changes in schedules, etc. Every evening she took the phones and plugged them in by her bed so her kids couldn't use them at night. She soon realized that her children's friends' parents didn't have the same policy. The phones were often buzzing all through the night with incoming texts. Her daughters were relieved of the pressure to stay in constant contact when they were trying to sleep.

Draw up "contracts" with your children explicitly laying out rules limiting the time they can spend on their phones. In her piece for *The Atlantic*, psychologist Jean Twenge wrote that, based on her research, the best advice she could give for a happy adolescence would be this: "Put down the phone, turn off the laptop, and do something — anything — that does not involve a screen."[118]

Set a Good Example

The American Academy of Pediatrics suggests that parents limit their own media use, thereby setting a good example for kids. Setting limits on screen time will be difficult for children who've grown up watching their parents constantly on their phones, tablets, and other devices. If you want to be the primary influence in your children's lives, you'll need them to pay attention to you. Start by paying enough attention to them.

In 2018, a Louisiana schoolteacher asked her second-grade students to write an essay about an invention they wished had never been created. She posted a photo of one of the essays on social media, and it quickly went viral. Along with a drawing of a cellphone crossed out, the student wrote: "I don't like the phone because my parent [sic] are on their phone every day … I hate my mom's phone and I wish she never had one."

Use Filters
As also discussed under "Solutions, Tips, & Tools" in the chapter on pornography, there is filtering software parents can install on digital devices that can greatly decrease the likelihood of accessing inappropriate material. There are also settings that allow different levels of internet access for different family members. The American College of Pediatricians suggests that parents consider a program that will allow them to monitor their children's online activity. They also recommend checking the parental control settings on their children's devices, which may allow parents to set time limits.

Manage Apps
Look for internet filtering software that allows parents to set parameters for app installation. Some software allows parents to block their kids from downloading apps entirely. *PC Magazine* analyzed such software in its report "The Best Parental Control Software of 2018."[119]

There are multiple apps available for smartphones that allow parents to monitor phone usage, see where their kids are, with whom they're communicating, and block objectionable websites. Tomsguide.com explains and ranks parents' options in its report, "Best Parental-Control Apps 2018."[120]

Writing at Breakpoint, John Stonestreet advises parents to check their children's phones specifically for affinity-based (or "Amino") apps. "If you find them, delete them, and then schedule dedicated time to talk with your child about what they've seen."[121] More information about "Amino" and other apps can be found at the website Axis.org. According to its website, Axis provides "insight into pop culture, technology, and media" from a Christian perspective.[122]

For Social Media

Oversee Social Media Accounts

Leonard Sax believes it's imperative for parents to know what their children do online, including social networking sites. He dismisses the concern some parents have about violating privacy. "You wouldn't let your fifteen-year-old daughter, much less your ten-year-old daughter, go to a college fraternity party by herself. By the same token, although for different reasons, you should not allow your daughter to engage in online social networking without your supervision."[123]

Be "friends" with your children on Facebook and "follow" them on all social media. At the same time be aware that it's not uncommon for teens to set up other accounts under different names as a way of avoiding detection by parents. Remember Leonard Sax's advice above that parents, with their children's knowledge, should oversee their online activities.

As Breakpoint's John Stonestreet writes, "Don't let anyone tell you that taking control of your child's digital behavior is somehow mean or overbearing. We have to protect our kids from digital predators just as we would a predator on the street. Both can and do kill. Your teen's safety and wellbeing are more important than any online community."[124]

The ChurchPOP website reported the story of a priest from Norfolk, Virginia, who sent out this tweet: "Dear Parents: Get Snapchat off of your kids' phones. Now. Don't ask. Just do it. Let them hate you. That will pass. Love, a priest who hears their sins."[125]

Protect Privacy

The American College of Pediatricians urges parents to make use of the privacy settings on social media sites. Privacy settings should be configured so that photos and information are only accessible to people your children know.

Talk with your teens about not divulging their passwords to anyone except you. Advise them not to share anything online that they would not want to be made public. Make sure your kids know never to share personal information (such as a phone number or a home address) with anyone online. And always be aware that most major social media sites, including Facebook, Snapchat, Twitter, and Instagram require users to be at least thirteen years old.

Be Aware of Sexting

Talk About It

Sexting has become too common for Christian parents to ignore. At an appropriate age or when you allow your children to have smartphones, discuss the practice with them, including the moral issues at play. Urge them to share with you any sexting incidents or issues they encounter. As with so many problems facing parents and their children, making rules and encouraging child-parent dialogue are critical.

Use Software

Leonard Sax recommends installing software that sends every photo taken on a child's phone to the parents' phone, in real time.[126] Sexting is too widespread, too tempting, and too potentially dangerous *not* to do everything possible to prevent it. (See info above on software and blocking technologies.)

Other Forms of Popular Entertainment

Do Your Research

Books, music, television, movies, and video games aimed at children and young adults often contain messages that are directly opposed to Christian teaching. Focus on the Family's website PluggedIn.com provides parents with detailed information that will help determine what's appropriate and what's not.

Limit Time

For children under the age of two, the American College of Pediatricians discourages the use of *all* screens, including televisions, phones, and tablets.[127] Parents should instead encourage the use of toys that foster creativity, such as blocks and crayons. For older children, ACPeds recommends limiting media exposure for entertainment purposes (television, movies, video games) to one hour or less per day.

Check Ratings

Be aware of the video game rating system and know the ratings of the games your children play. Parents should know that pornography can be embedded and accessed through a variety of video games. Video games with higher ratings have increased violent and sexual content. A number of websites offer parents great information on video games. Focus on the Family has a "Parents' Guide to Video Games." Christian Spotlight's "Guide to Games" is another good resource, as is the website ChristCenteredGamer.com. Common Sense Media provides parents with detailed descriptions of video games, along with suggested age ranges.

Quieting the Noise

Unplug

The American College of Pediatricians suggests that parents consider "unplugging" the whole family periodically — no TV, no tablets, no computers, no phones.[128] Choose a regular time, such as an evening or afternoon each week. Family vacations are ideal opportunities to go screen-free. And family dinners should always be free of digital distractions!

Be Creative

Encourage screen-free forms of entertainment, especially activities that involve physical activity. Have family game nights, or take bike rides or walks through the neighborhood together. Look for places to take nature walks or hikes as a family. And although listening to music may not be silence, the right kind of music can almost be a silence of its own, capable of taking us away from the world and toward God.

CHAPTER 4
SEX

As Christian parents, we want our children to understand sex differently than the rest of the world. We want them to understand and affirm chastity, knowing why it's important. We want them to appreciate sex as a gift from God to be shared within the context of marriage.

But maybe, like many Christian parents, you think that's an almost impossible ideal. Without a doubt this is an area where the world is going to work against you. The authority and influence you've been honing will be sorely tested by virtually every worldly exposure to sex your child experiences.

Just imagine that an alien suddenly dropped into our world to find out what our society thinks about sex. He'd observe how sex is presented in the TV shows we watch, the movies we go to see, the magazines and books we read, and what we look at on our computer screens and smartphones. Maybe he'd go to a high school and sit in on a sex education class to learn what kids are taught about sex. It's not hard to figure out what his conclusions would be.

He'd assume that everyone's "doing it," that there aren't any consequences (or none that anyone worries about ahead of time), that it's apparently enjoyable but not meaningful, that marriage has nothing do with it (if he'd even come across the concept of marriage), that there's no moral component (if he'd come across the concept of morality), and that there's no connection between sex and planning a family.

If we let the world raise our kids, they, too, will end up believing what the alien would: that sex is purely an act of pleasure, without meaning or consequence, to be engaged in without restriction (except perhaps regarding the use of contraception).

That's a far cry from the truth about sex according to the Church — which is pretty simple. Sex is intended for people who are married (marriage being the union of one man and one woman), and it has two purposes: to bind a husband and wife together and to make babies.

But you might be surprised at how few children — including Catholic and other Christian children — know and believe this. The National Survey of Youth and Religion (NSYR), conducted between July 2002 and April 2003, examined the religious, family, and social lives of adolescents. Mark Regnerus, an associate professor of sociology and religion at the University of Texas, was a co-investigator for the study. His 2007 book, *Forbidden Fruit: Sex & Religion in the Lives of American Teenagers*, details the findings of that and similar research.

Among the questions teenagers were asked in the NYSR survey was: "Do you think that people should wait to have sex until they are married, or not necessarily?" Only 51.2 percent of Roman Catholic teenagers said yes, slightly less than the 51.9 percent of mainline Protestants who agreed. Mormon teens ranked the highest, at 77.3 percent, followed by 73.7 percent for Evangelical Protestants.[129]

In terms of actual practice, the statistics are dismal. In his later book, *Premarital Sex in America: How Young Americans Meet, Mate, and Think About Marrying*, co-authored with Jeremy Uecker, Regnerus writes that "among all emerging adult women [ages eighteen to twenty-three] in any form of romantic relationship, only about 6 percent are not having sex of some sort."[130]

The sad truth is that some young people never even hear

what the Church teaches about sex. A young woman, originally from South America, once told me about her experience teaching at a Catholic high school here in the United States. Her students didn't hide from her the fact that many of them were engaging in sexual activities. When she told them that it was against the teaching of the Church, they scoffed. "Maybe it is in your country," they told her, "but not here."

In fact, a Harvard study estimates that more than 40 percent of parents don't talk to their children about sex and, for those who do, it's usually after their children have become sexually active.[131]

It's up to us to make sure our kids know the real truth about sex according to the Church's teachings. But we can't stop there. Remember that our kids, like the imaginary alien, will be bombarded by explicit and implicit messages that say exactly the opposite. They have to know the truth *and* be prepared for the lies.

Sex Ed

Consider the sex education your child is likely to receive in school as part of his health class. (Maybe you're thinking that your child is immune because he attends a Catholic or Christian school; however, it's best to make no assumptions about any school's sex education curriculum.) Programs vary, but the vast majority of schools teach what's called "comprehensive" sex education, also called Sexual Risk Reduction (SRR). In a nutshell, students are presented with a laundry list of options for giving and receiving sexual pleasure. Birth control methods are covered, and often demonstrated, such as having students put condoms on bananas. The risks of pregnancy and the transmission of STDs are covered, too, with teachers urging "safer sex," e.g., the use of condoms. Abstinence is usually at least mentioned, but merely as one choice among many. The mention of abstinence may lead some parents to assume, mistakenly, that SRR programs are benign. As it turns out, Sexual Risk Avoidance (SRA) programs (formerly called abstinence-based programs) are much more effective, much more in line with Christian teaching, and unfortunately, much harder to find.[132] Statistics compiled by the National Abstinence Education Association (now called Ascend), indicate that compared to their peers, students in SRA programs are "much more likely to delay sexual initiation … [and] if sexually active, much more likely to discontinue or decrease their sexual activity."[133]

Dr. Miriam Grossman is a psychiatrist and author of the book *You're Teaching My Child What? A Physician Exposes the Lies of Sex Education and How They Harm Your Child.* I urge you to read this book, along with her first one, *Unprotected: A Campus Psychiatrist Reveals How Political Correctness in Her Profession Endangers Every Student.* Grossman explains how modern sex ed came to be, what its real goals are, and the philosophy behind it. We're not telling kids how babies are made: we're telling them about the joy of sex. Briefly, here's why: The Sexuality Information and Education Council of the U.S. (SIECUS) was the country's first modern sex education organization. It, along with Planned Parenthood and Advocates for Youth (AFY), are today's primary promoters and providers of comprehensive sex ed to schools. AFY describes itself as a "trendsetter in cultural advocacy," working "to promote effective adolescent reproductive and sexual health programs and policies in the U.S."[134] SIECUS, which sounds official but is a privately-run organization, was founded in 1964 by Mary Calderone and other followers of Alfred Kinsey. Kinsey, of course, found fame as a sex researcher after publishing *Sexual Behavior in the Human Male* and, later, *Sexual Behavior in the Human Female.* As Grossman writes, "Kinsey's findings spawned a revolution and transformed western culture. The problem is, Kinsey's 'research' was fundamentally flawed."[135] According to Grossman, Calderone "found fault with the model used in school-based programs [at the time] because they focused on preventing pregnancy and venereal diseases. Calderone believed that when the negativity of sex educators is added to society's repressive morality, the result is too many *no's.*[136] She and her associates, therefore, set out to change young people's attitudes about sex. The goal was no longer to keep kids safe and healthy: it was to promote a secular, amoral view of sex.

Grossman explained to me in an interview for *Salvo* magazine that "From its inception, it was about changing society. The goal was to get rid of the constrictions and inhibitions of traditional sexual morality — in other words, the Judeo-Christian tradition of sexuality. That is the root of modern sex education, and that is what it still is today. It's not about health, it's about promoting a specific worldview."[137]

You only have to look at the *Guidelines for Comprehensive Sexuality Education*, published by SIECUS in 2004, to understand that worldview. From the introduction: "In a pluralistic society, people should respect and accept the diversity of values and beliefs about sexuality that exist in a community. ... Young people explore their sexuality as a natural process in achieving sexual maturity." Although SIECUS hasn't updated the Guidelines, its website is certainly up to date when it comes to progressive thinking. Here's their thinking about sex education being a human right: "Young people, like all people, have the right to autonomy over their bodies — to be fully in charge of their health and well-being regardless of anyone's opinions, values, beliefs, or desires."[138] And their stance on abortion couldn't be more clear: "There are millions of reasons why a person might choose to have an abortion. And any one of them is 100% valid."

Apparently, when it comes to teaching kids about sex in school there should be no judgments made because it's only natural that they act on their sexual urges!

In some schools, sex education isn't relegated to high school. The SIECUS *Guidelines* provide specific bullet points for sex educators working with children starting in kindergarten. Here's a sampling of what they recommend for discussion with children ages five to eight:

- Both boys and girls have body parts that feel good when touched.[139]

- Vaginal intercourse — when a penis is placed inside a vagina — is the most common way for a sperm and egg to join.[140]

- Some people are homosexual, which means they can be attracted to and fall in love with someone of the same gender.[141]

- A family consists of two or more people who care for each other in many ways.[142]

- Many people live in lifetime committed relationships, even though they may not be legally married.[143]

- Two people of the same gender can live in loving, lifetime committed relationships.[144]

- Touching and rubbing one's genitals to feel good is called masturbation.[145]

Do we seriously want our first-graders hearing about this, let alone from a teacher in a classroom surrounded by other children? The following are some recommended talking points from SIECUS for children ages nine to twelve:

- Some people are bisexual, which means they can be attracted to and fall in love with people of the same or another gender.[146]

- Children may have a mother and a father, two mothers, two fathers, or any other combination of adults who love and care for them.[147]

- Most boys and girls begin to masturbate for sexual pleasure during puberty.[148]

- A woman faced with an unintended pregnancy can carry the pregnancy to term and raise the baby, place the baby for adoption, or have an abortion to end the pregnancy.[149]

It's probably time for a deep breath! SIECUS not only recommends that third-graders be introduced to the concept of abortion, they suggest presenting it in a morally neutral way. For children ages twelve to fifteen, here are a few of the suggested topics:

- Many scientific theories have concluded that sexual orientation cannot be changed by therapy or medicine.[150]

- All societies and cultures have transgender individuals.[151]

- Values should be freely chosen after the alternatives and their consequences are evaluated.[152]

- No one has the right to impose their values on others.[153]

- Masturbation, either alone or with a partner, is one way people can enjoy and express their sexuality without risking pregnancy or an STD/HIV.[154]

- Some sexual behaviors shared by partners include kissing; touching; caressing; massaging; and oral, vaginal, or anal intercourse.[155]

- Young people can buy nonprescription contraceptives in a pharmacy, grocery store, market, or convenience store.[156]

- Some methods of contraception, such as condoms, can also prevent the transmission of STDs/HIV.[157]

- Individuals need to critically evaluate messages received from different sources and establish guidelines for their own behavior.[158]

- All people, regardless of biological sex, gender, age, ability, and culture are sexual beings.[159]

Apparently, middle schoolers are sexual beings, and *no one* has the right to impose their values on them, including their parents.

Here's what SIECUS recommends discussing with high school students ages fifteen to eighteen:

- As society builds a better awareness and understanding of gender identity, transgender individuals may be more accepted and face less harassment and violence.[160]

- Most women need some clitoral stimulation to reach orgasm.[161]

- Some people use erotic photographs, movies, art, literature, or the internet to enhance their sexual fantasies when alone or with a partner.[162]

- Some people continue to respect their religion's teaching and traditions but believe that some specific views are not personally relevant.[163]

This means that teachers are to tell students that they may or may not continue to respect what their religion teaches and that they can pick and choose their beliefs. And while they're at it, they might want to take a look at pornography!

STDs

Now you know what your children might encounter in their school's sex education programs. Here's some information they're *not* likely to get.

According to the Centers for Disease Control, every year there are ten million — ten million! — new cases of sexually transmitted diseases among our sons and daughters who are fifteen to twenty-four years old. The CDC reports that as of 2017, half of the 20 million new cases of sexually transmitted diseases reported each year were among young people ages fifteen to twenty-four.[164]

The number one sexually transmitted disease in this country is HPV, the human papillomavirus. There are several different strains of HPV, some of which we now know cause different types of cancer, including cervical cancer and cancers of the head and neck. Many people with HPV don't have any symptoms and don't even know they have it. According to one published study, almost half of girls who have had sex with only one partner have HPV.[165] Certain strains of HPV can be passed from a mother to her baby. For the record, condoms don't protect against many strains of HPV. Condoms protect against some strains, but not all. And the HPV vaccine? The same. Even with the vaccine, it's possible to contract the strain of HPV that causes cervical cancer.[166]

Another "common" STD, according to the CDC, is chlamydia. In 2013, there were nearly one million cases among fifteen to twenty-four-year olds. If our daughters are among that million, it could mean they'll never be able to have kids of their own.

There are now drug-resistant strains of gonorrhea, so in some cases it cannot be cured. And of course there's HIV/

AIDS, herpes, genital warts, and syphilis.

As for those condoms your kids will likely be encouraged to use if they have sex, a study by the National Institutes of Health determined that condoms provide 85 percent risk reduction against HIV.[167] Would you want your child to go skydiving if you were told that an average of fifteen out of one hundred parachutes don't open? That same NIH study was "unable to determine the effectiveness of condoms when it comes to other STD's." Meaning, condoms can at best *reduce* the risks of transmitting STDs and becoming pregnant.

Emotional Fallout
Maybe some readers have heard about hormones that are released during sex, sometimes called the "chemistry of sex." It's relatively new science, and it's interesting. During sex, a hormone called oxytocin is released, primarily in females. (Small amounts are released in males, too, but without any significant effect.) One of the things oxytocin does is lower a woman's defenses. It's sometimes called the "cuddle hormone." It leads a woman to trust her partner, whether her partner is deserving of trust or not. It causes her to bond with him. In a nutshell, it makes her more likely to fall in love. In males, the primary hormone released during sex is dopamine, which causes euphoria or happiness.

This is important information to understand. Due to hormones, a female can begin to develop a chemically driven bond with her partner. This is not a bond based on emotional connection, or on caring deeply for her partner, or on whether her partner is a nice guy who really cares about her.

In *You're Teaching My Child What?* Dr. Grossman tells the story of Kayla, a college student who started to drink and smoke pot until the wee hours of the morning. She would sleep all day, and by the time she came to Dr. Grossman for counseling, she'd missed two weeks of classes. It turns out that Kayla had begun hooking up with a guy who lived down the hall. The more often they had casual sex, "the more she needed to be with him. In spite of herself, she had feelings for him, and couldn't help wondering if he cared for her, too," Grossman writes. Despite the fact that David never contacted her except when they hooked up, Kayla had become preoccupied by him and was unable to sleep or concentrate on school. "Kayla's female brain ... predisposed her to yearn for connection, communication, and approval. Her chemistry promoted attachment and trust of David."

According to this, the chances of a young woman finding Mr. Right for a husband go way up if she keeps sex out of the picture while she's single. Why? It's partially due to the fact that her judgment won't be clouded by a hormone-induced fog. Likewise, a young man, having exercised the discipline to wait, won't see his partner primarily as a sex object. Both men and women will have a much better chance of getting to know their partners on an emotional level, which will also make them better judges of character. They'll know their partners for who they are, not for the sexual pleasure they provide.

Another reason to wait is because if a relationship doesn't include sex, a breakup will likely be much less painful. That chemical bond, that special closeness, won't have to be severed. Breaking up is hard enough. But with sex in the picture, it's a much more serious business, with the potential for serious emotional problems, including depression. Dr. Grossman recounts the devastating effects of casual sex among her patients in her book, *Unprotected*. "Almost daily, I prescribe medication to help students, mostly women, cope with loss and heartbreak."[168]

Kristen Walker wrote a blog for the LiveAction website about her decision to become abstinent.

I was never what you'd call promiscuous, but nor was I what you'd call sexually moral. Because of my willingness to give of myself completely to men who weren't willing to give me the same, I lived a life of heartbreak and confusion. Finally, about four years ago, I noticed that every time I gave my heart away, I wasn't getting it all back. Every go-round, there seemed to be less and less of my heart to give. I was becoming less open, more guarded, even bitter. I could feel a wall growing around my heart, and it was thick and it was high. I knew that one day, God willing, I was going to have a husband. Did I want him to end up with the leftovers, the dregs? Did I want him to have to mount a high wall to get to my heart?" Walker was thirty-two years old at the time she wrote that, in what she describes as a loving, but abstinent, relationship, and happy about her decision. "I have felt my heart heal, and I know that the next time I give myself to someone, it will be on my wedding night, to someone I trust, who has given himself to me in turn."[169]

It's been said that young women have sex in order to get love, and that young men give love in order to get sex. The truth is that having sex won't make a guy love the girl he's with. It may make him want her, but not necessarily in the long term, and not in the way she really wants or needs. For most guys, having sex with a girl doesn't "take the relationship to a whole new level." It stops it in its tracks. It becomes all about the sex. And that means reducing women to mere objects.

Young people who follow the Church's teaching and don't have sex until marriage will know whether their boyfriend or girlfriend loves them for who they are. They'll also just plain know that person a whole lot better. That emotional intimacy will be the foundation of their marriage, which will then be strengthened by the intimacy that comes with a sexual relationship.

For parents looking to present this positive-but-countercultural message to their teens, authors John Stonestreet and Brett Kunkle put it beautifully in their book, *A Practical Guide to Culture*: "Embedded in God's design of humanity is a holistic union of men and women within the husband-wife context: they are intended to become 'one flesh.' This one-flesh union entails sexuality. The sexual desire men and women have for each other is a good thing. If God designed sex, it only makes sense that we look to Him for vision, guidance, and wisdom in this area."[170]

It can be difficult for parents who didn't live out the sexual morals and values they want to instill in their children. Some may want to consider this advice from the section of Focus on the Family's website called "Before the Talk: Dealing With Our Past": "You may feel like a hypocrite if you insist that your children avoid behaviors you engaged in. ... Assessing your child's age and maturity level, you can speak frankly with your child about the damage — initially and lasting — that resulted from such behaviors." Others may reasonably choose to keep their sexual histories private.[171]

Pregnancy and Abortion

The Centers for Disease Control reports that nearly half of all pregnancies in this country are unintended. For women nineteen and younger that rises to four out of five. It's really pretty simple: sex makes babies!

According to the Guttmacher Institute, at 2014 rates, one in twenty women will have an abortion by age twenty, about one in five by age thirty, and one in four by age forty-five.[172] That's a staggering statistic! And here's another: In 2014 there were nearly a million abortions performed in the United States.[173]

Let's imagine that our pretend alien is trying to decipher what society thinks about abortion. Maybe he's seen the episode of the TV show *Scandal* in which the main character is shown calmly aborting her child while "Silent Night" plays in the background. No big deal. Maybe he's seen the #shoutyourabortion campaign in which young women are encouraged to "own" their abortions. Maybe he's seen pictures of women wearing T-shirts that say, "I had an abortion." Maybe he'd think it is a sign of pride.

What he wouldn't see in newspapers, popular magazines, or TV shows, are depictions of what abortion looks, or more precisely, feels like for countless women. For the most part, neither have our daughters. Let's put aside for a moment the moral aspects of abortion and the Church's teaching about it and think about the "it's no big deal" message society tells our young people. Nothing could be further from the truth, and it's up to us to tell them.

Consider the story of Theresa Burke. When she was a graduate student in the field of psychotherapy, she led a weekly support group for women with eating disorders. During one session, a patient named Debbie confided that she was having flashbacks to an abortion she had several years before. The distress they caused was compounded by phone messages she was getting from her ex-husband, in which he called her a "murderer" and rehashed gruesome details of the abortion. After these phone calls, Debbie would often become suicidal and end up in the hospital emergency room. She was also severely anorexic.[174]

The revelation of Debbie's abortion led others to speak up. Beth Ann explained that she could understand how Debbie felt because she'd also had an abortion. Next was Diane, who, in the midst of a curse-laden rant against men, alluded to having had an abortion. Another patient, Judith, became so upset that she got up and left.

It turned out that six of the eight women in the eating disorders group had undergone abortions. "In subsequent discussions, all six women indicated that their abortions were perhaps the most difficult decisions they had ever made," Burke later wrote. "At the same time, however, they denied that their abortions had any significant effect on their lives."

Burke sensed that, as she put it, "a lot of unexplored and unresolved feelings were being denied, repressed, or suppressed." And because unexpressed emotions are often the key to treating eating disorders, Burke broached the subject of how to proceed with her supervising psychiatrist. She was instructed in no uncertain terms to drop it. Period. She was forbidden by her supervisor to explore the possibility of helping her patients by addressing their past abortions. Linking abortion to depression and other psychological disorders was prohibited.

But Burke couldn't forget what she'd learned in that support group. Having recognized that abortion was an issue for many women, she decided, after completing her training, to establish small, free support groups for women who had abortions. The sessions "were always filled, even though we never advertised," Burke told me in an interview for *Salvo* magazine. "It was all word of mouth."

Very quickly, she sensed that the women's pain ran very deep. "I even began to sense that therapy — coming in to discuss their abortions — actually made it worse. We now know from research that talk therapy does not always help victims of trauma." So Burke started Rachel's Vineyard, now one of the more well-known post-abortion healing programs consisting of weekend retreats for people suffering from the pain and guilt of abortion. Rachel's Vineyard, now a ministry of Priests for Life, currently holds 1,000 retreats a year, in forty-nine states and seventy countries.

Of course, we want our daughters to know that abortion is wrong. In addition, we want them to know that what the world will tell them about abortion is false and misleading. It is, of course, impossible to know whether every woman who has had an abortion suffers in some way afterwards. But we do know — and our daughters should be made aware — that many women do suffer afterwards.

Take Cynthia, for example. Cynthia is a psychologist who now works as a volunteer at Rachel's Vineyard retreats. At the time she had her abortions, she was strongly pro-choice. As a psychologist, she'd had her share of psychotherapy, and she didn't believe she'd suffered any emotional scarring as a result of her abortions.

But shortly after she became Catholic, a friend who knew about her past abortions urged Cynthia to attend a Rachel's Vineyard retreat. At first, Cynthia was skeptical and resistant, but she finally relented after deciding it would be a chance to learn more about this type of therapeutic intervention for post-abortive women.

It proved to be much more than that. In an interview with me for *Salvo* magazine, she described the retreat as a life-changing experience. "It was so powerful that I made the decision to dedicate the rest of my career to helping women heal psychologically from abortion. I had no idea I was harboring a very sizable amount of pain — a real psychological woundedness — around my own abortions. The pain that came out of me was astounding."

Michaelene Fredenburg was eighteen years old when she had an abortion, and she recalls being completely unprepared for the emotional fallout. She was overwhelmed by a range of feelings, from anger to profound sadness. She suffered in silence for years before finally seeking help from a trained counselor.

Fredenburg has since written a book called *Changed: Making Sense of Your Own or a Loved One's Abortion Experience.* She has also started an outreach called Abortion Changes You, which she describes as "an invitation for people from all faith backgrounds who have experienced abortion — men, women, grandparents, siblings, other family members, and friends — to discover that they are not alone and that healing resources are available."

The Abortion Changes You website provides a place where people can share their experiences, safely and anonymously. There are common threads running through many entries: guilt, depression, drug and alcohol abuse. Many entries are heartbreaking to read. "I cried for twenty years," reads one. "My inside is like a giant hole," reads another. "I don't think I will ever be able to be me again." Many people express anger that they weren't given information about the psychological impact abortion can have.

In truth, pro-abortion groups often misleadingly downplay the emotional effects of abortion. One of the Frequently Asked Questions on Planned Parenthood's website is "How will I feel after my abortion?" Here's their answer:

> You may have a range of emotions after having an abortion. Most people feel relief, but sometimes people feel sad or regretful. This is totally normal. If your mood keeps you from doing the things you usually do each day, call your doctor or nurse for help. You can also call Exhale or All-Options for free, confidential, and non-judgmental emotional support after an abortion — no matter how you're feeling.[175]

Actress Jennifer O'Neill went public a few years ago about the abortion she had when she was twenty-two years old. In her book, *You're Not Alone: Healing Through God's Grace After Abortion*, O'Neill speaks openly about both the emotional and the physical scars she suffered as a result of her abortion. She is now a spokesperson for Silent No More, a campaign to make people aware of the suffering abortion can cause — to both women and men — and to inform them that help toward healing is available.

In his book *Arrogance: Rescuing America from the Media Elite*, author and former CBS News correspondent Bernard Goldberg explains why the truth about the after-effects of abortion aren't addressed by the media. For example, he writes that, in 1990, *Los Angeles Times* reporter David Shaw wrote a 12,000-word, four-part series on how the media covers abortion. Shaw's conclusion, as Goldberg summarizes it, was that "the culture of the American newsroom is so overwhelmingly pro-choice that the media have a tough time covering the story fairly."[176] Goldberg also notes that

Shaw's reports were almost universally ignored, notably by the media itself.

Professional organizations, too, tend to downplay the possibility that abortion has any serious after effects. In August 2008, the American Psychological Association's Task Force on Mental Health and Abortion (TFMHA) presented its findings on post-abortion trauma. This is from the APA's website: "[I]t is clear that some women do experience sadness, grief, and feelings of loss following termination of a pregnancy, and some experience clinically significant disorders, including depression and anxiety. However, the TFMHA reviewed no evidence sufficient to support the claim that an observed association between abortion history and mental health was caused by the abortion per se, as opposed to other factors."[177]

In 2011, the Academy of Medical Royal Colleges surveyed multiple studies and found similar results, such as this one: "A woman with an unwanted pregnancy is as likely to have mental health problems from abortion as she is from giving birth."[178]

According to Burke and others in the field with whom I spoke, typical manifestations of post-abortion trauma include depression, anxiety, eating disorders, nightmares, and difficulty with intimacy. Some reactions are delayed for years; others are immediate. "I think most women, if they knew it was going to impact them in such a negative way, would never, ever in a million years have chosen to have an abortion," Burke told me. "Having a baby would have been a breeze compared to trying to deal with all the problems that were borne later."[179]

Our daughters should know that post-abortion suffering is overlooked in debates on the issue. It's generally unreported in the media, and unacknowledged by the culture. But it's a very real phenomenon, as the thousands of individuals who have found help and healing through organizations such as Rachel's Vineyard, Silent No More, and

Abortion Changes You could attest.

Our sons should know that men, too, experience post-abortion suffering. Writing for *Salvo* magazine, Terrell Clemmons cites Brad Mattes, a founding member of MAN (Men and Abortion Network). In his experience, anger is the most evident symptom of post-abortion trauma for men. "In addition, a man may turn to alcohol, drugs or overwork to dull the pain of knowing he participated in or was too 'weak' to prevent the death of his unborn baby."[180]

In their study, *Men's Mental Health and Abortion: A Review of the Research,* co-authors C. T. Coyle and V. M. Rue looked at a variety of research conducted on the subject of how abortion affects men. "Common findings among these reports include the following: evidence that abortion is not a benign experience for many men, … post-abortion ambivalence involving a variety of emotions, relationship difficulties, and an expressed need or desire for counseling."[181]

Rachel's Vineyard treats men as well as women for post-abortion suffering. Here is one testimonial on its website from Scott: "After struggling alone for years with the guilt and shame of my involvement with my girlfriend's decision to abort our child, I finally found a ministry that recognized my need to get help."[182]

In his book, *Peace of Soul,* Archbishop Fulton J. Sheen wrote about the modern-day obsession with sex. "The Victorians pretended it did not exist; the moderns pretend that nothing else exists." Promoting chastity in such aptly described circumstances is a tall order. The benefits of self-discipline, emotional well-being, freedom from disease and fear of unwanted pregnancy, along with future marital stability and satisfaction make instilling the Christian view of sex in our children well worth the effort.

SOLUTIONS, TIPS, & TOOLS

Do Your Sex Ed Homework

Find out what your children's school sex education curriculum is. Start by visiting the "Parents School Toolkit" section of the Ascend (formerly called the National Abstinence Education Association) website.[183] It's important to be prepared ahead of time, according to the NAEA's former president, Valerie Huber. "Don't just ask whether abstinence is taught or whether delaying sexual activity is promoted, because every teacher, no matter what curriculum is being used, will say 'yes,'" Huber told me.[184] She urges parents to ask to preview the curriculum, ask to see all handouts, and inquire what, if any, supplementary material will be used, including videos. If you decide to try to change a school's sex ed program, there's strength in numbers. Seek out like-minded parents and present a united front. Remember that there are many misperceptions about "abstinence-based" sex ed, including the often-repeated fiction that it doesn't work. The Ascend website includes a summary of twenty-three studies that show a positive impact on teens' sexual behavior from abstinence-based programs.[185] If you're not in agreement with your school's sex ed curriculum and it's not feasible to change it, insist that your child be excused from those classes.

Give Your Children the Facts

When it's appropriate, adolescents should know about the very real dangers of sexually transmitted diseases — not as a scare tactic, but as a reality check. The statistics provided earlier in this chapter come straight from the Centers for Disease Control website. They are simply the cold, hard facts.

The "chemistry of sex," the emotional bonding that results from a sexual relationship, is also key for adolescents to know about. When they're old enough, have them read Dr. Miriam Grossman's book *Unprotected* for real-life stories of how deeply young people suffer as a result of hooking up, breaking up, and assuming that there is such a thing as meaningless sex. As Christians, we wish the option of abortion didn't exist. But it does. Go beyond the moral teaching of the Church regarding abortion as the taking of an innocent life and make sure your kids know about the suffering post-abortive women and men often experience. Have them read *Fatherhood Aborted* by Guy Condon and David Hazard, and Jennifer O'Neill's book, *You're Not Alone: Healing Through God's Grace After Abortion*. It will help them understand this other facet of abortion and give them tools to guide and help friends considering that painful choice in the future.

Be Positive
Young Christians also need to understand abstinence and sex within marriage as *positives*. Author Peter Kreeft, in his book *Because God is Real*, talks about sacredness. "Sex is sacred because sex is not just *made* by humans but sex *makes* humans, makes more of those sacred things that we call human beings. ... There is only one reason why being unfaithful and giving your body sexually to many people is so wrong: because being sexually faithful and giving your whole body to one person is so right."[186]

Dawn Eden's book *The Thrill of the Chaste: Finding Fulfillment While Keeping Your Clothes On (Catholic Edition)* is a great resource regarding the positives of chastity. Rebecca Smith, writing about Eden's book for *Catholic Exchange*, summed it up like this: "Chastity is the ability to moderate our own sexual desires, and involves much more than simply saying 'no' to sex before marriage. In fact, chastity is all about saying 'Yes!' 'Yes!' to recognizing the inherent dignity and value in every person. 'Yes!' to acknowledging the power and purpose of God's design for the sexual act, and to valuing that act enough to wait for its rightful context. 'Yes!' to seeing through a society that tries to make a chaste person seem weak, self-conscious, afraid, and controlled by pointless, rigid rules."[187]

Writing in *Salvo* magazine, W. Knight (who writes anonymously with the goal of "integrating Christian faith and knowledge in the public square" at WinteryKnight.com) discussed some of the positives of chastity.[188] Some of his main arguments:

- Practically speaking, remaining chaste gives couples "space to seriously evaluate their suitability as marital candidates."

- Chastity "encourages the development of self-control."

- Chastity demonstrates a person's "desire and ability to provide for [another's] specific emotional needs."

- Couples who are chaste can't use sex as a method of conflict resolution.

Dr. Mike Artigues, a pediatrician who serves on the Board of the American College of Pediatricians, sums it up this way in an interview for *National Catholic Register*: "It's not a matter of saying 'no' to sex because it's bad. It's a matter of saying that there's a right time for it."[189] It's also reasonable to tell young people that abiding by the teachings of the Church when it comes to sex — a good in and of itself — is also likely to lead to better physical and emotional health.

There are even studies about the positives of waiting. A research team at Brigham Young University surveyed over 2,000 couples ranging in age from nineteen to seventy, comparing different outcomes such as communication, stability, and sexual and relationship satisfaction. All the outcomes were better for the couples who had waited for sex till after the marriage.[190]

Explain Why

Dr. Jenell Williams Paris is the author of *The End of Sexual Identity: Why Sex Is Too Important to Define Who We Are*. In an interview with *Relevant* magazine, she makes the case that Christians need more than rules in order to live out chastity. What's often missing, Paris believes, is a compelling story and an understanding of the "why's" behind the rules. She explains this by using the example of parents teaching their children to look both ways before crossing a street. "A young child may follow this rule solely because of the power of her parents' authority which is appropriate. As she grows, the child [continues to look both ways] but for a deeper reason that she owns for herself. She sees the broader context of traffic, understands the benefits and dangers and makes choices accordingly. Rules are external and authority-bound: Maturity requires knowledge of *why* to do the right thing, not just what the right thing is."[191]

Every parent knows that each child is unique. Some may be more naturally inclined to accept rules, and others are inclined to resist authority. The facts and figures about the very real dangers of sexually transmitted diseases, the risks of unplanned pregnancy, the potential for serious emotional trauma, and the pain of abortion provide a basis for discussing the "why's" for doing the right thing, as Dr. Paris puts it. The main point here is that parents need to be the primary educators of their children when it comes to sex. If children are never told what the Church teaches by their parents, they may never find out. And if they're not forewarned about the untruths they'll hear in school, from friends, on TV, via social media, and from all around them, they'll be unprepared to hold firm to the truth.

Seek Support

Sometimes, though, good parenting isn't enough. There were other interesting findings from the National Survey of Youth and Religion (NSYR) that Mark Regnerus wrote about in his book *Forbidden Fruit: Sex & Religion in the Lives of American Teenagers.*

Despite the dismal overall results (if you recall, only 51.2 percent of Catholic teens believe sex should be reserved for marriage, etc.), among adolescents who reported attending weekly religious services (not broken down by affiliation), 66.2 percent said they believe in waiting for marriage. The numbers jumped considerably among teens who reported being in church *more* than once a week: 83 percent of them believe in waiting for marriage before having sex. The bottom line? The more involved adolescents are in their churches, the more they believe in what those churches (and their parents) teach about abstinence till marriage. Based on his research, Regnerus concludes that what matters most is what he calls "high religiosity" and teens being immersed in "religious plausibility structures." Here's how he defines that: "A network of like-minded friends, family and authorities who (a) teach and enable comprehensive religious perspectives about sexuality to compete more effectively against ubiquitous sexually permissive scripts, and (b) offer desexualized time and space and provide reinforcement of parental values."[192]

Here's the takeaway: First, the more involved adolescents are in their churches, the more they believe in what those churches teach about chastity. Second, parents are rarely able to do the job alone. Like it or not, to some extent, children *are* raised by the "village" around them. Seek out others who reflect your values — like-minded friends and children's playmates, along with extended family — and make them part of your children's lives.

CHAPTER 5
PORNOGRAPHY

Maybe you're thinking this subject doesn't apply to you. You'd never allow your children to view pornography! Please continue reading. Don't make the mistake of thinking your child will never be exposed to it — either by accident or intentionally. Pornography is too easy for a child to stumble upon or seek out, and it is toxic. Beyond the fact that it obscures the truth of God's plan for sex, it can do quite a lot of harm in ways you might not expect.

A lot has been written about the "pornification" of popular culture, and with good reason. TV commercials for Axe deodorant and Victoria's Secret are the equivalent of what once would have been considered soft-core porn. I remember seeing copies of *Maxim* magazine scattered around a teen clothing store for shoppers to peruse. It's difficult to find a television sitcom or drama these days where sex isn't a plot line or a laugh line. Sex is everywhere. So it's no surprise that many teens — and their parents — have a "no-big-deal," morally indifferent attitude about pornography. Some have a wink, wink, nudge, nudge, boys-will-be-boys attitude when it comes to porn. Others assume everybody looks at it. These are the sorts of attitudes our children are surrounded by and from which they need our protection.

When *Playboy* magazine was first published in 1953, it marked a kind of coming-out party for porn, which until then had been largely undercover, if not underground. As time went on, "men's magazines" became more mainstream. "Soft core" porn is considered to be a form of free speech, according to the Supreme Court.[193] Some consider it nothing more than a form of artistic expression. It's likely all these factors have helped pave the way for the "hard core" variety to become so easily available with the click of a mouse or the touch of a smartphone.

Parents need to educate themselves about the damage pornography can do to young people, understand how easily accessible porn has become, and learn how to protect their children from it.

What's Wrong

Perhaps the first thing to acknowledge about viewing pornography is that it's wrong, according to the Church. In 2015, the U.S. Conference of Catholic Bishops issued a pastoral letter on pornography called *Create in Me a Clean Heart.* Here is a small portion of it:

> The *Catechism of the Catholic Church* defines pornography this way:
>
>> Pornography consists in removing real or simulated sexual acts from the intimacy of the partners, in order to display them deliberately to third parties. It offends against chastity because it perverts the conjugal act, the intimate giving of spouses to each other. It does grave injury to the dignity of its participants (actors, vendors, the public), since each one becomes an object of base pleasure and illicit profit for others. It immerses all who are involved in the illusion of a fantasy world. (2523)

The moral status of pornography is clear from this

passage: producing or using pornography is gravely wrong. It is a grave matter by its object. It is a mortal sin if it is committed with full knowledge and deliberate consent. Unintentional ignorance and factors that compromise the voluntary and free character of the act can diminish a person's moral culpability. This sin needs the Lord's forgiveness and should be confessed within the Sacrament of Penance and Reconciliation. The damage it causes to oneself, one's relationships, society, and the Body of Christ needs healing. Pornography can never be justified and is always wrong.[194]

This clear and strong teaching from the Catholic Church has unfortunately not gotten through to the present culture. A Barna Research Group survey found that a majority of teenagers believe that "not recycling" ranks as worse on the immorality scale than viewing porn.[195]

Most young people have likely never been taught that viewing pornography is wrong. They probably take their cues from society, where "soft core" porn is seemingly everywhere. The only way our kids will know it's wrong is if we tell them. The culture around us definitely won't be sending them that message. It's up to us, when the time is right, to talk to our kids not only about the dangers of porn but the fact that it's just plain wrong.

Maybe "Soft Core" Isn't So Bad

Dr. Judith Reisman has been sounding the alarm about the negative effects of pornography since the 1980s, long before the widespread use of computers and other online devices. Her book *"Soft Porn" Plays Hardball* addressed the issue of children and pornography in 1991, when exposure was primarily through magazines:

It is generally accepted that premature exposure to

sexually stimulating images affects children negatively. ... The "fantasies" displayed in soft porn magazines are too often blueprints for brutal crime. The Pollyannas who argue that sadosexual pictures do not encourage and stimulate anger, aggression, and crime in some children and adults should, as they say, wake up and smell the coffee. Or, start reading the reports — like the FBI study which found that nearly all serial rapist-murderers admit pornography as their major interest.[196]

As long ago as 1970, the "President's Report on Obscenity and Pornography" cited the fact that young children use pornography to educate themselves about sex.[197] In his 1979 book *Teenage Sexuality*, Dr. Aaron Hass discussed the widespread use of pornography by children. At that time, *Playboy* magazine was the source for most of the children he interviewed. He writes: "Many adolescents turn to movies, pictures and articles to find out exactly how to have sexual relations. ... The children said 'you really learn a lot ... in the *Playboy* advisor ... I wanted to learn the real facts. ... These magazines give me something to go by.'"[198]

The evidence of negative effects has been documented of such "soft-core" pornography on both adults and children. Now consider where we are almost fifty years later and the "education" any child with a laptop, tablet, or smartphone can get viewing "hard-core" moving images of what most Christians would consider sexually deviant behavior.

Not Your Father's Porn

The Witherspoon Institute, a research center based in Princeton, New Jersey, spent two years studying the social costs of pornography. A wide range of experts in various fields, hosted by professor Robert P. George, met to present research on the subject of the problem of pornography in society. The project's overview statement addressed the issue of how pornography has evolved:

> Today's pornography ... is increasingly of the hard-core variety, meaning the presentation, through moving images, of real sexual acts, in which the focus of attention is on the sexual organs of the participants, male or female, heterosexual or homosexual, adult or child. ... A few futile attempts are made to protect children, but these attempts cannot withstand the tide of permissiveness. In a culture in which pornography is permitted to flourish ... children cannot be insulated even from its direct effects, much less its indirect ones."[199]

Not only is today's porn significantly more graphic, and therefore more harmful, it's also significantly more accessible. Thanks to the digital age, pornography is available in virtually any home with access to the internet and in the hands of anyone with a laptop, tablet, or smartphone. According to statistics cited by Pat Fagan, director of the Marriage and Religion Research Institute, 75 percent of porn-watching is on smartphones.[200]

What's the Harm?

Dr. Jill Manning is the author of *What's the Big Deal About Pornography? A Guide for the Internet Generation.* She's also a therapist who specializes in pornography issues and problematic sexual behavior. Exposure to pornographic images, according to Manning and other mental health professionals, can have a lasting negative and even traumatic impact on the brains and psychological well-being of children and adolescents. Dr. Manning should know since many of her patients are just such casualties. Manning doesn't hold back when it comes to what she thinks about pornography: "I believe pornography is the most successfully marketed insult and attack on our divine nature as human beings that has ever existed," she writes. "There's never been anything so calculated and widespread and so effective at reaching so many people at such a young age."[201]

Here's what we parents need to know. Young people who are exposed to pornographic images at a formative stage of their growth as sexual beings will often come to see sexuality as completely disconnected from relationships, and certainly disconnected from any spiritual context. Another danger is that they learn how to objectify human beings, seeing others in a context devoid of feelings, personalities, and needs.

Here's more from the US Conference of Catholic Bishop's pastoral letter on pornography: "Being exposed to pornography can be traumatic for children and youth. Seeing it steals their innocence and gives them a distorted image of sexuality, relationships, and men and women, which may then affect their behavior. It can also make them more vulnerable to being sexually abused, since their understanding of appropriate behavior can be damaged."[202]

In Dr. Manning's experience, young people often first turn to pornography for sexual information. They hear a word or a term they're too embarrassed to ask about, so they go online. That can lead them into a world of outrageously graphic and often perverse demonstrations of sexual behavior for which they have no frame of reference. What they end up getting is misinformation because, as Manning told me in an interview for *Salvo* magazine, "there are so many lies inherent in pornographic material about bodies, about relationships, about gender, about sexual response. It's all one big fat lie."[203]

But pornography doesn't just misinform, it harms. According to a study in *Child Abuse Review*, "Particularly among younger children, exposure to pornography may be disturbing or upsetting." And, especially among boys and young men, "consumption intensifies attitudes supportive of sexual coercion and increases their likelihood of perpetrating assault."[204] The American College of Pediatricians warns both parents and pediatricians about the harms of pornography for children. "Children suffer many negative effects due to modern society's exposure to and acceptance of pornography. These negative effects include mental disturbance and unrest for the school age child, including acting out and violent behavior."[205]

Who's Watching

If you picture dirty old men when you think of who's watching online porn, it will surprise you to learn that the largest group of viewers of pornography using the internet is children between the ages of twelve and seventeen. Those statistics come from the non-profit advocacy organization Enough is Enough, citing a variety of studies.[206] There are additional disturbing pieces of research data. The average age of first exposure to online porn is estimated to be eleven. Among fifteen- to seventeen-year-olds, 80 percent have had multiple exposures to hardcore pornography. A 2014 Canadian study found that 40 percent of boys between the ages of four and eleven have sought out online pornography, many admitting that they do so frequently.[207] Another Canadian study found that among thirteen and fourteen-year-olds, 90 percent of males and 70 percent of females reported accessing sexually explicit media content at least once. There is evidence that much exposure is accidental, often happening in the course of doing homework. According to a 2005 study published in the journal *Pediatrics*, 42 percent of internet users aged ten to seventeen surveyed said they'd seen online pornography in a recent twelve-month span.[208] Of those, 66 percent said they did not want to view the images and had not sought them out. A 2018 study reveals that 57 percent of teens search out pornography at least monthly. Fifty-one percent of male students and 32 percent of female students viewed porn before the age of thirteen.[209]

It's difficult to know exactly how many pornographic websites are in operation, but according to one survey, such sites receive more traffic each month than Amazon, Netflix, and Twitter combined. Considering that, according to one estimate, there are currently over four million pornographic websites in operation,[210] that shouldn't be surprising. The Marriage and Religion Research Institute reports that 70 percent of American college students watch pornography.[211]

Many children stumble upon explicit material while doing otherwise innocent internet searches, doing homework, or simply by opening email. According to statistics compiled by GuardChild, 70 percent of children ages seven to eighteen years old have inadvertently been exposed to online pornography.[212]

As Dr. Manning puts it, "It is strange how the virtual world has seemingly escaped the societal standards accepted in various public squares even though the internet has been alive and well since the early 1990s."[213]

Some of Dr. Manning's patients report first encountering pornography at the age of five or six. Manning told me about one of her patients — now a grown man — who is struggling with same-sex attraction. He firmly believes he is straight, and he wants to get married and have a family. But his first sexual experience was with homosexual pornography — beginning at the age of nine. In Dr. Manning's experience, pornography shouldn't be taken lightly. "It's not something you dabble in for a few years and then clean up your act before you get married. This will handicap your ability to be intimate in marriage. If you desire a satisfying sexual experience with a spouse someday, this is a surefire, fast track way to ruin that."

Of course, not every child or teenager who is exposed to pornography will return to it habitually, but many do, putting them at risk for a variety of negative consequences. Young viewers of pornography are statistically more likely to engage in sexual intercourse earlier than their peers. According to Dr. Manning, there is also evidence that young people viewing pornography are less likely to desire marriage and having a family. "They start letting go of some of those goals and dreams," she told me. "They begin to think that marriage is just a hassle and a hindrance, and that they'll attain greater sexual satisfaction in life if they're engaged in casual encounters. And they are certainly at an increased risk for developing sexual compulsions and addictive behavior." Studies have shown that habitual users of pornography often need harder and more deviant material over time to achieve satisfaction.[214]

There is documented evidence that children and adolescents directly exposed to pornography are also more likely to overestimate the prevalence of less common practices such as group sex, bestiality, and sadomasochistic activity. Exposure to unhealthy sexual norms in the form of pornography has the potential to permanently imprint sexual deviance on a child's brain.

The pornography widely available today is in a whole new league from the "men's magazines" of an earlier era. Dr. Manning believes that most teenage boys, for example, would be completely unfazed by a *Playboy* magazine from the 1960s. "Their reaction would be that they see that at the mall, or on TV, that it's no big deal. Today's pornography has become deviant, vile and graphic. Young people are witnessing rape, torture, and all kinds of degrading material."

Women and Children at Risk
One of the presenting scholars for the Witherspoon Institute's study of the impact of pornography was Dr. Ana Bridges, a psychologist at the University of Arkansas. Her research exposed another disturbing aspect of today's porn. A study of fifty top-selling adult videos revealed the prevalence of a theme: women were overwhelmingly depicted as victims of aggression. And if that weren't enough, only a tiny percentage of those aggressive acts elicited a negative response from the victim. Dr. Manning, in her testimony to the Witherspoon Institute, carried that theme a step further. "I am witnessing

more female adolescents tolerating emotional, physical and sexual abuse in dating relationships, feeling pressure to make out with females as a way to turn guys on ... and normalizing sexual abuse done to them because they see the same acts eroticized in pornography. After all, how bad can it be if the larger culture around you finds abusive and demeaning acts a turn on?"

The US Conference of Catholic Bishop's pastoral letter gets specific when it comes to the risks to girls. "For girls, an over-sexualized society in general and pornography in general can contribute to low self-esteem, eating disorders, and depression."[215]

As noted earlier, many children come across pornography online accidentally. Operators of pornographic websites often use words and terms a child might innocently put into a search engine. Author Christine Sanderson, in her book *The Seduction of Children*, notes that such child-friendly terms include Barbie, Pokémon, Disney, and My Little Pony.[216] Another common practice is to use domain names similar to legitimate ones, even official government agencies.

No Safety Net

Enough Is Enough is a non-profit organization founded in 1994 with the goal of making the Internet safe for children. One of its stated objectives is keeping pornography off children's digital screens. A paragraph on Enough.org sums up where things stand at the moment: Today any child with unrestricted internet access is just a mouse click away from viewing, either intentionally or accidentally, sexually explicit material online, from adult pornography ... to prosecutable material depicting graphic sex acts, live sex shows, orgies, bestiality, and violence.[217]

Although a minor may not legally purchase a pornographic magazine at a newsstand, or be allowed in to watch an R-rated movie in a theater, or rent an "adult" video, the same protections do not apply on the internet.

SOLUTIONS, TIPS, & TOOLS

Take Responsibility

The first thing parents need to understand is that the responsibility for protecting our children from pornography lies with us. Many parents, accustomed to the safety nets in place for print and broadcast outlets, simply don't realize that they bear this burden. In fact, statistics from the Pew Research Center show that the use of parental controls and filters has *decreased* over the last few years. In 2005, more than half of American families used filters to block potentially harmful online material.[218] But by 2016, only 39 percent made use of parental controls for their teens' online activities, with a paltry 16 percent doing so for mobile devices.[219] Parents are, in effect, the only line of defense between children and pornography, at least wherever there's a digital device and internet access. Dr. Manning, most of whose clients are Christians, believes that parents need a wake-up call. Many don't know what's out there, and how easily it can be accessed. Many don't know that their kids might come across it by mistake. Many have the attitude that it simply couldn't — or wouldn't — happen in their homes.

Get Educated

Enough is Enough has produced a program for parents called "Internet Safety 101."[220] This multi-media resource includes a DVD series, containing strikingly candid interviews with teenagers discussing their experiences with pornography. One teenage boy talks about not wanting to have relationships with girls after watching pornography, but just wanting to have sex with as many girls as possible. A teenage girl discusses the negative impact it had on her relationships with boys, and on her self-respect. Another boy comments on the difficulties of avoiding it on the internet, and the brilliant marketing strategies of pornographers. "It will find you," he warns.

One courageous mother tells a cautionary tale. She and her husband discovered that their then-eleven-year-old son had been getting up in the middle of the night to watch pornography. When she and her husband checked the computer's history, they found that he'd visited over 900 porn websites. At the age of twenty, he is still trying to overcome his addiction. Sadly, he is far from alone. As Dr. Manning told me, "I believe we are raising a whole generation that believes sex is a spectator sport."[221]

The "Internet Safety 101" program includes information on steps parents can take to protect their children. "Become a good cyber-parent, or put your children at risk," is the advice of Donna Rice Hughes, president of Enough is Enough.

Talk About It

James Dirksen has been on Enough is Enough's Internet Safety Council for several years. He also founded, and for a period of time ran RuleSpace, a company that built pornography filtering technology. Beyond his fourteen years of experience working in the field of internet filtering, he's a father of six with a personal interest in the topic. In an interview for *Salvo* magazine, Dirksen told me that communication is paramount.[222] Parents must let their children know that there are dangerous and inappropriate things on the internet and to be careful when using it. The communication must run both ways, with children agreeing to talk about anything they see online that makes them feel uncomfortable. Children should also be aware that they might stumble across it by mistake and that friends might try to show inappropriate material to them. Parents should advise their children about what to do in both of those circumstances.

Dr. Manning agrees and believes that parents need to discuss the existence and the dangers of pornography with children, much as they do when it comes to drugs and alcohol. Children need to know, in an age-appropriate way, that such images can turn them away from God's plan for the love between a husband and wife and that pornography is not an accurate representation of sex.

When your child gains access to a digital device — their own, a friend's, or at school — it is time to start the discussion. The organization Educate and Empower Kids has published a book called *How to Talk to Your Kids About Pornography*. They recommend parents start by explaining what pornography is. The definition you use will obviously depend on your child's age and his or her level of understanding. Here's the official definition they use: "The portrayal of explicit sexual content for the purpose or intent of causing sexual arousal. In it, sex and bodies are commodified (made into a product for sale) for the purpose of making a financial profit."[223] Simpler definitions they suggest, presumably for young children, include these: "Pornography is pictures or videos of people with little or no clothes on." And "Online pornography usually shows videos of people having sex."[224]

Another book to consider for young children is *Good Pictures Bad Pictures: Porn-Proofing Today's Young Kids* by Kristen A. Jenson and Gail Poyner. It's a read-aloud book with the goal of installing an internal filter in children's brains to keep them safe from the poison of pornography.

Use Available Protections and Filters

Since most of the digital devices kids use are portable (laptops, smartphones, and tablets), parents should consider device filtering (as opposed to filters that work at the modem level). There are several companies that offer this. Educate and Empower Kids names these specifically as the best internet and phone filters of 2018:

- K9Webprotection.com
- Netnanny.com
- Covenanteyes.com
- Norton Family
- Qustodio

- KidLogger
- McAfee
- Wigito
- Surfie by Pure Sight[225]

Parents should research the options and features offered by each company so they can choose the one that best fits their family's needs.

Many North American mobile carriers offer free filtering for smartphones. Again, parents should research what filters each company offers, and decide if they're sufficient.

Although Dirksen acknowledges that no system is perfect (hence the need for communication), filtering technology is better than it's ever been. "If parents have thought about installing these things but hesitate because they think they're not perfect, they're not thinking it through. You wouldn't not put a life jacket on your child in a canoe just because life jackets don't always work."[226]

Use "Dumb" Phones

Here's what Patrick Fagan, director of the Marriage and Religion Research Initiative at The Catholic University of America, wrote on the topic: "[S]avvy parents — and even savvy teenagers — will switch to dumb phones. Giving a teenage boy a smart phone is installing a porn-shop in his pocket … and a very alluring shop it is too: cheap (free) porn, immediately available, and anonymous."[227]

CHAPTER 6
CONSUMERISM

For parents trying to raise children who are grounded in the faith and striving for spiritual fulfillment — rather than worldly — living in our material world can be an enormous stumbling block. It's easy to lose sight of what a consumer-driven culture ours has become and how much that affects our everyday decisions and thinking.

We're bombarded with the message that having more stuff will make us happy. Commercials and ads do this openly and aggressively, yet we're still seduced. Peer pressure, heightened by social media, is more insidious but no less potent. If adults are susceptible, imagine how easy it is for our children to grow up in thrall to materialism.

Pope Francis addressed this issue at a Mass in St. Peter's Square, saying: "Whenever material things, money, worldliness, become the center of our lives, they take hold of us, they possess us; we lose our very identity as human beings." The pontiff added that when materialism takes over, we "end up becoming self-absorbed and finding security in material things which ultimately rob us of our face, our human face."[228]

We need to look no further than the Gospel of Matthew to read what Jesus said on the subject: "Do not lay up for yourselves treasures on earth, where moth and rust consume and where thieves break in and steal; but lay up for yourselves treasures in heaven, where neither moth nor rust consumes and where thieves do not break in and steal. For where your treasure is, there will your heart be also" (Mt 6:19–21).

Making an Idol of "Stuff"

In a culture where acquisitiveness is extolled and celebrated (think of the Kardashians) it can be difficult to avoid making an idol of "stuff." Though there's nothing new about envy, the desire to "keep up with the Joneses" is compounded by knowing so much about them thanks to social media. Whether it's parents comparing their lives with their Facebook "friends," or kids seeing how they stack up against the latest Snapchat and Instagram postings, it can be hard to avoid falling into the sin of covetousness. We want a house just like our neighbor's. Our kids want the designer sneakers their friends have.

Like our first parents, it's hard not to be tempted into believing that we know best. It's hard not to think that stuff — a new car, the latest tech gadget, a bigger house — is what will make us truly happy. For one thing, it's hard to escape knowing about all the stuff out there that we ourselves don't have. For another, there simply is so much stuff that surrounds us. So many of us have most or all of our material needs met, yet we desire even more.

According to *The Wall Street Journal*, data collected from the Commerce Department in 2011 indicates that Americans spend $1.2 trillion on non-essential goods and services every year.[229] That's a lot of money for a lot of stuff that we don't need, such as candy, jewelry, and alcohol. It adds up to 11.2 percent of total consumer spending, compared to 4 percent in 1959 (adjusted for inflation).

Here's a noteworthy passage from the book *Affluenza* by John De Graaf and David Wann: "Since World War II, Americans have been engaged in a spending binge unprecedented in history. We now spend nearly two-thirds of our $11 trillion economy on consumer goods. For example, we spend more on shoes, jewelry, and watches ($100 billion) than on higher education ($99 billion). We spend as much on auto maintenance as on religious and welfare activities. Nearly 30 percent of Americans buy Christmas presents for their pets."[230]

Here are two more telling statistics from the 2014 version of this book: America has more shopping malls than high schools, and for 93 percent of teenage girls, shopping is their favorite activity.[231]

As a culture, we've come to associate happiness with possessions. In their book *A Practical Guide to Culture: Helping the Next Generation Navigate Today's World*, authors John Stonestreet and Brett Kunkle address this issue. "Happiness hasn't always had the contorted meaning it now has in contemporary culture. The 'pursuit of happiness' in the Declaration of Independence wasn't the unbridled pursuit of affluence, pleasure, and personal satisfaction. Happiness was found in a life well lived, characterized by wisdom, virtue and character."[232]

Compared with other periods in history, most Americans today live with an unprecedented abundance of material possessions and comforts. In their book, *Lost in Transition: The Dark Side of Emerging Adulthood*, authors Christian Smith, Kari Christoffersen, and Hilary Davidson asked emerging adults what would define "the good life." "[F]or most, financial success, material acquisition, and consumer enjoyment" topped the list.[233]

But, as the saying goes, money can't buy happiness. Though Americans have more disposable income and material goods — bigger houses, more cars, and more clothes when compared to our predecessors — all that "stuff" doesn't seem to be making us happier. According to Madeline Levine in her book *The Price of Privilege*, "the highest rates of depression, substance abuse, anxiety disorders," and general unhappiness are found in the preteens and teens of affluent, well-educated families.[234] Researchers have found that the most troubled adolescents often come from afflu-ent homes.[235] Affluence and the acquisition of "stuff" do not lead to happiness.

Parent Peer Pressure

The effects of peer pressure aren't limited to children. I remember the first over-the-top birthday party my then-three-year-old and I attended for her nursery school class-mate. There must have been thirty preschoolers in atten-dance, along with their parents, for a gymnastics frolic at the local Y, followed by cake and ice cream. The gift table was overflowing (so much stuff!), and the whole event felt over-whelming, even unpleasant. Yet, it was hard not to walk away wondering about what to do when our turn came around.

Dr. William Doherty, Director of the Marriage and Family Therapy Program at the University of Minnesota, talks about the issue of parent peer pressure in his book *Take Back Your Kids.* "When every other child in the school has an expensive birthday party, we want nothing less for our own son or daughter. We justify it as something nice for our child, but in truth we don't want to be out of step with our peers."[236]

Many parents end up making excessive purchases for their children simply because they're worn down by inces-sant demands. But parents often get into what Doherty calls a "consumer frenzy for their children," in effect, competing with other parents over the latest hard-to-find toys. We've all seen news stories showing parents fighting over the last Tick-le Me Elmo (or other popular plaything-of-the-moment) left on the toy store shelf. We act like we're in competition for a Parent of the Year Award — as if being a good parent equates with getting our kids "stuff."

The other aspect to this is that our children notice. "We adopt new technologies, such as cellphones and fax machines, with unprecedented speed. We upgrade our computers when the old ones work fine," Doherty writes. "We upscale our transportation by purchasing expensive sports utility vehicles that are not really any better for most of us than a regular automobile. ... The status and expense of a product or service comes to signify its quality or usefulness. Our wants become our needs in an escalating pattern of acquisition. And our children notice all this and learn."[237]

A 2016 British survey found that nearly half of the parents they talked to felt pressure to buy things for their children in order to "keep up with the Joneses."[238] The top two items fueling the parental peer pressure were technology-related goods such as cellphones and tablets, followed by clothing.

Advertising and Kids

In 2010, researchers Anna McAlister and T. Bettina Cornwell conducted a study to assess levels of brand recognition in children ages three to five. They found that contrary to prior research, children that young can and do understand brands. Reading what they concluded beyond that is truly startling:

> Preschoolers can and do judge others on the basis of brand use. ... The present results show that children as young as three willingly judge their peers. They see other children as popular or unpopular, fun or boring, because of the brands they use. Such judgments suggest that, at an early age, children attribute great importance to the use of branded products to cultivate and promote self-image. These findings, therefore, seem to flag an early emergence of materialism among preschool children.[239]

Doherty recounts two grandparents being both amazed and appalled when shopping with their granddaughter. "She marches down the aisles, thoroughly familiar with the merchandise, pointing to items and saying, 'I want this' and 'I want this one too, but I don't want that one.' A discriminating shopper at age three!"[240]

A Kaiser Family Foundation study concluded that kids ages eight to eighteen watch on average about four and a half hours of television per day (thanks in part to television being ever more accessible online and on mobile devices). Based on information from the Federal Trade Commission, the Campaign for a Commercial-Free Childhood estimates that children between the ages of two and eleven view over 25,000 advertisements a year on television alone.[241] All those commercials have the potential to turn kids into what Dr. Thomas Lickona calls "'wanting machines' who are never satisfied with what they have."[242] As mentioned earlier, Lickona is a developmental psychologist and author of several books, including *How to Raise Kind Kids* and *Raising Good Children*. "Our souls aren't made for stuff,"[243] as he puts it, despite what the world would have us and our kids believe.

Consider these staggering statistics about marketing to children compiled by the Campaign for a Commercial-Free Childhood:

- Companies spend about $17 billion annually marketing to children, a staggering increase from the $100 million spent in 1983.

- Children under fourteen spend about $40 billion annually. Compare this to the $6.1 billion four to twelve-year olds spent in 1989. Teens spend about $159 billion.

- Children under twelve influence $500 billion in purchases per year.

- This generation of children is the most brand-conscious ever. Teens between thirteen and seventeen have 145 conversations about brands per week, about twice as many as adults.[244]

Clothing and Modesty

The issue of dressing modestly (which relates mostly to girls) could fit into multiple chapters in this book. But considering the fact that most mothers will at some point find themselves shopping for clothes with their daughters, we'll tackle it here. Rebecca Hagelin, a nationally syndicated columnist and author of *30 Ways in 30 Days to Save Your Family*, writes about the challenges of finding clothing that's appropriate for girls but still appealing. If you haven't visited a mall recently and stepped into a store selling clothes for young girls and tweens, you're in for a shock. Thongs, bare midriff tops, tiny skirts, and skin-tight pants are being marketed and sold to girls as young as seven and eight. It's just another example of the sexualization of children.[245]

If our girls haven't come across such items in advertisements, it's likely they've seen plenty of movie and television characters (from both fictional and "reality" shows) dressed, as Hagelin puts it, like "street-walkers." And even if they haven't seen such clothing in movies or on TV, chances are, they've seen it on their friends and classmates in person and on social media. The combination of peer pressure with advertising and marketing makes the issue of girls dressing modestly one that most parents of daughters will have to confront.

SOLUTIONS, TIPS, & TOOLS

Talk About "Stuff"

We should teach our kids, early on, that "stuff" isn't what makes us truly happy. As adults, we know that the novelty of a new gadget soon wears off. "Help your kids reflect on their own experience of this," Dr. Lickona told me in an interview.[246] Talk with them about how many once "favorite" toys and gizmos sit in the back of a closet, long forgotten.

With young children, parents can start the conversation

by watching the VeggieTales episode titled *Madame Blueberry*. With wit, humor, and fun songs, it manages to convey the emptiness of acquiring "stuff" and the deep contentment that comes from gratitude and from having what Madame calls "happy hearts."

Just Say "No!"

Michele Borba is the author of *Unselfie: Why Empathic Kids Succeed in Our All-About-Me World*. Among her suggestions for how to avoid raising materialistic monsters is to learn how to say "No." Parents should resist the urge to give in to a child's materialistic desires, and shouldn't feel guilty about it either. Parents should explain why it's important not to focus on stuff. And be prepared for resistance.[247]

Authors John Stonestreet and Brett Kunkle second this: "Resist the urge to buy things just because your kids ask for them. Of course, blessing your kids with gifts is good, but never if the purpose is to appease them, bribe them, or compensate them for your lack of time or attention. When you do say no, explain why."[248]

Talk About What Truly Makes Us Happy

"We should help our children realize what truly does make us happy: loving relationships, developing our God-given talents, doing work we can take pride in, growing closer to God through prayer, and acts of kindness and helpfulness in our family and beyond,"[249] Lickona advises. Also, it helps if children learn that from their own first-hand experience when possible. He told me about one father who found that volunteering in a soup kitchen with his fifteen-year-old son helped curb his constant requests for the latest "stuff."

Of course, there are some things that do make us happy and enrich our relationships with others. Lickona suggests discussing with children what kinds of things are "life- and growth-enhancing," and which aren't. Games that can be played as a family, a bicycle that can be ridden with friends, books that enrich the imagination, and music that nourishes the soul are all good examples.

Encourage Gratitude

While gratitude may not be the antonym for materialism, it may be the antidote to it. Writing for *Mother Magazine*, Lickona recommends developing rituals that encourage gratitude in children. At dinnertime, go around the table for what he calls a quick round of "gratefuls," where everyone names something they're grateful for that day.[250] Or, during bedtime devotions, be sure to include prayers of thanksgiving.

No Comparisons Allowed

Make it a family policy that no comparisons to others are allowed. Lickona even suggests posting a sign on the fridge that reads: NO COMPARISONS.[251] And though comparison is normal for kids to do ("John or Jane has a new fill-in-the-blank"), we should teach our children that comparisons make us unhappy; for one thing, there will always be somebody who has more than we do!

Face Peer Pressure Head On

Discussing peer pressure openly with your kids will help them understand it, recognize it, and handle it. Social media sites and apps such as Snapchat, Instagram, YouTube, and Facebook make peer pressure even tougher on today's children. Constantly knowing what others are doing, what friends they're hanging out with, and what clothes they're wearing isn't healthy. If kids know how to identify peer pressure when it happens, they'll be better at resisting it.

Keep Advertising at Bay

To avoid turning kids into "wanting machines," Lickona advises parents to keep Madison Avenue out of their living rooms as much as possible. Limit television viewing. Ideally, choose programs the family can view and discuss together.

Use streaming sites that don't have commercials. "In today's world, families that want to be their child's main moral educator must commit to being countercultural in big ways, and that includes taking the road less traveled when it comes to making relationships, not media consumption, paramount in family life," according to Lickona.

Talk Before You Shop Together

Author Rebecca Hagelin believes it's important for mothers to discuss the issue of dressing modestly with their daughters ahead of any shopping trip. "Let your daughter know, in loving but uncompromising terms, what clothing will and will not be acceptable,"[252] she writes.

Hagelin's conversation with her own daughter (repeated many times) went something like this: "Kristin, God made you lovely and special. You are someone to be respected. And I, as your mom — the one who loves you more than anyone else in the world could possibly love you, and who deeply understands the need and desire to feel attractive — commit to you that I'm going to help make sure that you dress in a way that shows your inner character, reveals your true beauty, individuality, and the fact that you are not just a toy."[253] They agreed on one rule when shopping: before buying something, they would both have to like it. Her daughter wouldn't try to convince Hagelin to buy clothing she thought was inappropriate, and Hagelin wouldn't force her daughter to wear something she thought was "dorky."

Be Good Role Models

As we know, parents are as susceptible to consumerism as children. Sometimes it's hard to watch other parents buy their children whatever they ask for and not feel pressure to do the same. Parents should consider their own motives when making purchases and resist the urge if it's simply to keep up with the Joneses.

As Dr. Lickona explains it: "Obviously, we can't expect

our kids to stand up to peer pressure if we don't model that — if we don't stand up to pressure we feel from our peers, namely, other parents who are getting their kids whatever they nag them for, or from the consumerist culture that surrounds and bombards us. ... Very often, kids look back with pride at having had parents who had the guts to buck the culture in these ways."[254]

Borba recommends spending time, not money, with your kids. Go bike-riding together, or to a park or museum. Bake together or play games. "Show your kid the alternative to a consumeristic life." And remember the example you set. Think about whether your children would describe you as someone who believes it's who you are — not what you own — that's important. "Be the nonmaterialistic model you want your kids to copy."[255]

Be Careful at Christmas

If there's one holiday that's been overtaken by consumerism, it's Christmas. For children in particular, it's become a season of getting more than giving. Dr. Lickona suggests that families start traditions that shift that focus. He recommends contributing as a family to a charity. "Just considering the possibilities will be an education in how many groups in your community and around the world are doing wonderful work to improve the lives of people in need," he explained. "As parents, we can — and must — create a family culture that instills a better understanding than that of what God wants us to do with our lives. There's no better time than Christmas to bring that into focus, starting with gratitude for the gift God gave us that day — and how we can try to give back."[256]

The American College of Pediatricians offers suggestions on its blog to help shift kids' thoughts from getting to giving during the holiday season:

- Find ways to give back locally by helping in a local soup kitchen or animal shelter, or whatev-

er other community service organizations are
available.

- Encourage your children to reach out to individuals who need help, like the child in the
  cafeteria who always sits alone.

- Teach children the importance of giving and
  helping within their families, by sharing toys or
  helping someone else with their chores.[257]

FINAL THOUGHTS

This book is for those of you who've made the decision to raise your children as faithful Christians. Hopefully you've gained some insights into the stumbling blocks you'll run into, how to be prepared for them, how to prepare your kids for them, and how to work around them. Keep in mind that the ultimate goal is to instill the faith, otherwise all the protections you put in place, all the precautions you take, all the world-proofing you do, and all the loving, authoritative parenting you demonstrate will be in vain: your most pivotal role is as primary teachers of the faith.

We wouldn't expect our children to grow up understanding the value of being kind to others if we ourselves weren't. The same applies to any virtue: courtesy, honesty, compassion, patience, diligence, humility, self-control, stewardship, and modesty. The best way to instruct children in learning virtue is to live them out with our children as witnesses. Children learn best by example. If they see us being kind, they learn kindness, and so on.

The same applies to faith. When our children see us demonstrating our faith, they learn faithfulness. If we don't witness to our children by actions and by words, how can we expect our children to understand or care about God?

If we send our children to Catholic or Christian schools, religious education classes or Sunday School, but don't reinforce the most critical lessons in our homes, how can we expect our children to take them seriously? If we leave religious education solely up to others, why would our children believe Jesus is any more important than, say, algebra or grammar? Whether we send our children to Catholic schools, Christian schools, or public schools, or do the schooling ourselves, forming them in the faith is our responsibility.

Peter Kreeft is a Catholic author and professor of philosophy at Boston College. His book *Before I Go: Letters to Our Children about What Really Matters* is a series of short "letters" addressed to his children and grandchildren. In a stream-of-consciousness style, he talks to them about what he calls "the most valuable life lessons I have learned."

Here are some excerpts:

> [W]e can *know* God and not just know *about* Him. We can be His friends. . . . He's actually there, and we actually meet Him when we pray, whether we feel that or not, and He actually *does stuff to us* when we pray, whether we feel it or not.[258]

> Everything that exists, from yourself to a grain of sand, is God's love made visible, made incarnate — love in the form of creation. The words He spoke to create everything in the universe — "let it be" — were the words of love. He loved stuff into being.[259]

> Do you wonder what I pray for you every day? It's the same thing my father prayed for me every day. That you should be happy, really, truly happy. And therefore good, since there is no other way to be really, truly happy. And therefore close to God, since He is where all goodness comes from.[260]

These are the kinds of things we should be saying in our own way to our children every day, at every opportunity, at every teachable moment.

The Catholic Church calls the family the "domestic

church." It's within the context of family that children first have the opportunity to understand who God is, to hear from their parents what God means in their lives, and to observe their parents living out a life of faith.

These two passages from the *Catechism of the Catholic Church* (which could be applied to any Christian home) sum it up nicely:

> In our own time, in a world often alien and even hostile to faith, believing families are of primary importance as centers of living, radiant faith. For this reason, the Second Vatican Council, using an ancient expression, calls the family the *Ecclesia domestica*. It is in the bosom of the family that parents are by word and example ... the first heralds of the faith with regard to their children. (1656)

> The Christian home is the place where children receive the first proclamation of the faith. For this reason the family home is rightly called "the domestic church," a community of grace and prayer, a school of human virtues and of Christian charity. (1666)

SOLUTIONS, TIPS, & TOOLS

Get Help
If the idea of taking responsibility for forming your children in faith seems overwhelming, ask for help. Get copies of the lessons your children are being taught in Sunday School or religious education. Not only will they serve as good refresher courses for you, they'll help you start conversations that can reinforce life's most important teachings.

For Catholic adults who want to brush up on their faith, there is Bishop Robert Barron's book, *Catholicism: A Journey to the Heart of the Faith*. It's available with a study guide and workbook, or as a DVD set.

Focus on the Family offers a series called *TrueU*, which consists of DVDs and study guides. It's recommended for individuals and/or groups who want to strengthen their faith. Focus on the Family's website has a page called "Teaching Kids About God" that offers a variety of resources, including recommended books.

For Catholic families, there are home-based religious education curricula available for purchase. FamilyFormation. net, for example, offers weekly home lessons for parents instructing children from pre-K through grade six.[261]

Pray Together

A book that was highly recommended to me on the topic of family prayer is *A Short Guide to Praying as a Family*, written by the Dominican Sisters of Saint Cecilia in Nashville. Archbishop Charles J. Chaput of Philadelphia writes this in the foreword: "Helping children learn the habit of prayer thus becomes one of the most important lessons a family can share."

The United States Conference of Catholic Bishops has on its website a section called "Tools for Building a Domestic Church."[262] Many of the suggestions, not surprisingly, focus on prayer and apply to all Christians. Pray together as a family. Say grace before meals. Nurture a habit of bedtime prayers with children. Pray a family Rosary. Encourage unstructured prayer.

On its website, Focus on the Family has a section called "Praying Together As a Family." Here's one of their suggestions: "Teach your kids that prayers don't have to be long, formal and fancy. When you're together, offer up short, spontaneous, conversational prayers."

Let Your Children See You Praying

"Allow your children to witness you in private prayer," says the USCCB. What could be more meaningful and inspiring to a child than to see his mother or father praying? In a pamphlet called "10 Things That Make for a Great Catholic Dad," Cory Busse seconds the idea: "Get 'caught' praying, and pray with your children — over meals, at bedtime, anytime. Praying with someone is a pretty intimate act."[263]

Focus on the Family echoes those thoughts: "So let your children hear *you* bringing *your* needs and requests before the Lord in an attitude of humble expectancy."[264]

Rebecca Hagelin describes the moment when, as a young girl, the sound of someone weeping led her to her parents' bedroom door. It was open just enough for her to peer in and see her father, a pediatrician, kneeling at his bed crying and praying for a young patient of his. "I stood there in awe of this brilliant man who realized that he needed to go to the Great Physician for help," she told Crosswalk.com in an interview. "That tremendous moment of faith — when he never knew I was watching — impacted me for the rest of my life in terms of where I place my faith."[265]

Go as a Family to Church Regularly

For Christian families, there should be no question about it: we go to church together. For me, the habit of going to church with my family every Sunday became a habit of the heart, probably reinforced by the fact that my father was a church organist and choir director!

For Catholics, it's important to attend weekly Mass and go to confession regularly as a family. "Our kids are watching, and they will do what we do," Cory Busse writes. "They're watching if we're ambivalent about getting to Mass. They're watching if we're checking the time during the homily, calculating whether or not we'll make it home before kickoff. But the good news is, they're also watching when we do things right!"

The USCCB urges parents to make the sacraments a regular celebration by taking the whole family to confession and Mass. They also make a point of reminding parents of the importance of not missing Mass if at all possible. If we want our kids to know that going to Mass is important, then we have to make it a priority. Think of the message conveyed to children when parents send them to Sunday school and religious education classes, but don't go to church themselves!

Be Involved in Your Church and Encourage Your Children to Do the Same

We've seen evidence in previous chapters that young people who are involved in their church beyond attending Sunday services are more likely to accept its teachings and incorporate them into their lives. The USCCB suggests that parents participate in lay ministries and other activities and encourage their children to do so as well. So find out what activities are available at your parish and encourage your children to get involved.

Make Use of Summer Retreats and Christian Camps

In a piece for *National Catholic Register*, several Catholic parents who send their kids to public schools were interviewed about how they keep them faithful.[266] Many of the parents make a point of having their children attend summer retreats that focus on faith formation. Some have found programs in their area run by Jesuits, Franciscans, or Opus Dei, whereas others have found summer youth retreats at Catholic colleges and universities.

The TheologyDegrees.org website offers suggestions for what they call "The 25 Most Amazing Christian Summer Camps."[267] No doubt pastors, priests, other parents and members of your congregation can offer recommendations.

Start Family Traditions Based on Liturgical Seasons

For Catholics, celebrating the seasons of the liturgical year in our homes is a great way for children to understand that the practice of our faith doesn't begin and end at the church door. Kendra Tierney's book, *The Catholic All Year Compendium: Liturgical Living for Real Life*, is about just this. She shares ideas for celebrating Catholic seasons and feasts incorporating foods, activities, stories, and decorations.

Advent wreaths with candles are a great way to mark the preparation for the coming of Jesus. There are many sources online for Scripture readings and prayers to be said at the lighting of each candle on the Sundays in Advent. You might also buy or make an Advent calendar that contains Bible verses that tell the story of Christmas.

A Christmas creche can be a beautiful and memorable reminder of what the holiday is truly all about. I remember reading about a family whose Christmas morning tradition was to pray together around the creche before any gifts were opened.

Lent is another season easily observed in the home by making sacrifices as a family and fasting together. I know one family with four children whose Lenten tradition is to learn, as a family, a new psalm each year, memorizing and reciting it line by line each night.

Talk About God with Your Children

There's no question that going to church as a family is important because children learn by example. But what may be just as important is explaining to children *why* we do these things. Children need to understand the meaning behind going to Mass or attending Sunday service — why it matters — so they don't dismiss it as merely a habit or family tradition.

In addition, if we want our children to be truly faithful, they need to understand that God isn't only for Sundays. So follow another suggestion from the USCCB: "Talk freely about the presence of God in the joys and sorrows of your life."[268]

Remember the instructions Moses gave the Israelites in the Old Testament: "You shall therefore lay up these words

of mine in your heart and in your soul. ... And you shall
teach them to your children, talking of them when you are
sitting in your house, and when you are walking by the way,
and when you lie down, and when you rise" (Dt 11:18–19).

RESOURCES

General

Recommended Books:
Before I Go: Letters to Our Children about What Really Matters by Peter Kreeft

Recommended Websites:
https://www.familyformation.net/

http://www.usccb.org/beliefs-and-teachings/vocations/
parents/tools-for-building-a-domestic-church.cfm

Parenting

Recommended Books:
Take Back Your Kids: Confident Parenting in Turbulent Times by William Doherty

Childhood Unbound: Authoritative Parenting for the 21ˢᵗ Century by Ron Taffel

The Collapse of Parenting: How We Hurt Our Kids When We Treat Them Like Grown-Ups by Leonard Sax

Cleaning House: A Mom's 12-Month Experiment to Rid Her Home of Youth Entitlement by Kay Wills Wyma

How to Raise Kind Kids and Get Respect, Gratitude, and a Happier Family in the Bargain by Thomas Lickona

Recommended Websites:
https://www.acpeds.org/the-college-speaks/position-statements/parenting-issues/the-benefits-of-the-family-table

https://www.acpeds.org/10-basic-principles-of-good-parenting-part-3

https://www.acpeds.org/parents/authoritative-parenting

Sex

Recommended Books:
You're Teaching My Child What? A Physician Exposes the Lies of Sex Education and How They Harm Your Child by Dr. Miriam Grossman

Unprotected: A Campus Psychiatrist Reveals How Political Correctness in Her Profession Endangers Every Student by Dr. Miriam Grossman

You're Not Alone: Healing Through God's Grace After Abortion by Jennifer O'Neill

The Thrill of the Chaste (Catholic Edition): Finding Fulfillment While Keeping Your Clothes On by Dawn Eden

Forbidden Fruit: Sex and Religion in the Lives of American Teenagers by Mark D. Regnerus

Because God is Real: Sixteen Questions, One Answer by Peter Kreeft

The End of Sexual Identity: Why Sex Is Too Important to Define Who We Are by Jenell Williams Paris

Fatherhood Aborted by Guy Condon and David Hazard

Recommended Websites:
American College of Pediatricians: https://www.acpeds.org/the-talk-for-parents-part-1#more-15225; https://www.acpeds.org/talking-to-children-about-sex; https://www.acpeds.org/sexual-responsibility-2/incidence-and-consequences-of-sexual-activity

Parents School Toolkit at Ascend (formerly the National Abstinence Education Association): https://weascend.org/wp-content/uploads/2017/10/ascendparentsschooltoolkit-min.pdf?x69289

Centers for Disease Control/STDs: http://www.cdc.gov/std/

Dr. Miriam Grossman: http://www.miriamgrossmanmd.com/

Rachel's Vineyard: http://www.rachelsvineyard.org/

Abortion Changes You: http://www.abortionchangesyou.com/

Silent No More: http://www.silentnomoreawareness.org/

Pornography

Recommended Books:
What's the Big Deal About Pornography? A Guide for the Internet Generation by Dr. Jill Manning

Soft Porn Plays Hardball by Judith Reisman

Teenage Sexuality by Aaron Hass

How to Talk to Your Kids About Pornography by Educate and Empower Kids

Good Pictures Bad Pictures: Porn-Proofing Today's Young Kids by Kristen A. Jenson and Gail Poyner

Recommended Websites:
American College of Pediatricians: https://www.acpeds.org/the-college-speaks/position-statements/the-impact-of-pornography-on-children

www.enough.org

www.AFO.net

www.netnanny.com

www.K9Webprotection.com

www.covenanteyes.com

www.Internetsafety.com

https://family.norton.com/web/

http://www.usccb.org/issues-and-action/human-life-and-dignity/pornography/index.cfm

Schools

Recommended Websites:

The Cardinal Newman Society: https://cardinalnewman-society.org/

The Cardinal Newman Society's K–12 Program: https://cardinalnewmansociety.org/program/k-12-program/

The Cardinal Newman Society's National Catholic Honor Roll: https://cardinalnewmansociety.org/catholic-ed-honor-roll/current-awardees/

The Cardinal Newman Society's Parent Guide: https://cardinalnewmansociety.org/principles-catholic-identity-education/parent-guide/

Focus on the Family's True Tolerance: www.true.tolerance.org

The Family Policy Alliance: http://familypolicyalliance.com/allies/

USCCB Catholic Schools and Parental Choice: http://www.usccb.org/beliefs-and-teachings/how-we-teach/catholic-education/upload/Our-Greatest-Inheritance.pdf

EWTN (on homeschooling): https://www.ewtn.com/library/HOMESCHL/CATHHS.HTM

Homeschooling Catholic: http://www.homeschoolingcatholic.com/links/curriculum/

Regina Caeli Academy: http://www.rcahybrid.org/#

Home School Legal Defense Association: https://hslda.org/

Home School Foundation: https://www.homeschoolfoundation.org/index.php?s=homeschool-resources

Association of Classical Christian Schools: https://classicalchristian.org/

Media

Recommended Books:
Girls on the Edge by Leonard Sax

30 Ways in 30 Days to Save Your Family by Rebecca Hagelin

American Girls: Social Media and the Secret Lives of Teenagers by Nancy Jo Sales

Be the Parent, Please: Stop Banning Seesaws and Start Banning Snapchat by Naomi Schaefer Riley

iGen: Why Today's Super-Connected Kids Are Growing Up Less Rebellious, More Tolerant, Less Happy — and Completely Unprepared for Adulthood — and What That Means for the Rest of Us by Jean Twenge

The Power of Silence: Against the Dictatorship of Noise by Robert Sarah and Nicolas Diat

Recommended Websites:
Parents Television Council: www.parentstv.org

University of Michigan Health System Television Guide: http://www.med.umich.edu/yourchild/topics/managetv. htm

PluggedIn: www.pluggedin.com

American College of Pediatricians information on media: https://www.acpeds.org/the-college-speaks/position-statements/parenting-issues/the-impact-of-media-use-and-screen-time-on-children-adolescents-and-families; https://www.acpeds.org/beware-of-media

Cyberbullying Research Center: https://cyberbullying.org/

Breakpoint's Guide to Amino Apps: http://www.breakpoint.org/free/, http://www.breakpoint.org/2018/04/breakpoint-delete-amino-musical-ly/

Internet Safety 101 (from Enough is Enough): https://internetsafety101.org/

Growing Wireless (resources & information for parents): http://www.growingwireless.com/

Axis (media, culture & technology from a Christian perspective): https://axis.org/

To download "A Parent's Guide to Amino Apps": http://www.breakpoint.org/free/

Common Sense Media: https://www.commonsensemedia.org/

Teen Safe: https://www.teensafe.com/

Tom's Guide to the "Best Parental Control Apps 2018:" https://www.tomsguide.com/us/best-parental-control-apps,review-2258.html

Focus on the Family's "Parents' Guide to Video Games:" https://www.focusonthefamily.com/parenting/kids-and-technology/parents-guide-to-video-games/parents-guide-to-video-games

Internet Filters and Monitoring Programs (recommended by ACPeds):

Net Nanny: https://www.netnanny.com/

Covenant Eyes: http://www.covenanteyes.com/

Screen Retriever: http://www.screenretriever.com/

My Mobile Watchdog: https://www.mymobilewatchdog.com/

Consumerism

Recommended Books:
Take Back Your Kids: Confident Parenting in Turbulent Times, by William Doherty

Lost in Transition: The Dark Side of Emerging Adulthood by Christian Smith

Raising Good Children: Helping Your Child Through the Stages of Moral Development by Thomas Lickona

How to Raise Kind Kids: And Get Respect, Gratitude and a

Happier Family in the Bargain by Thomas Lickona

30 Ways in 30 Days to Save Your Family by Rebecca Hagelin

A Practical Guide to Culture: Helping the Next Generation Navigate Today's World by John Stonestreet and Brett Kunkle

Affluenza: How Overconsumption is Killing Us — And How to Fight Back by John De Graaf and David Wann

The Price of Privilege: How Parental Pressure and Material Advantage Are Creating a Generation of Disconnected and Unhappy Kids by Madeline Levine

Unselfie: Why Empathic Kids Succeed in our All-About-Me-World by Michele Borba

ABOUT THE AUTHOR

As a contributor for the *National Catholic Register* and Senior Editor for *Salvo* magazine (and formerly as a columnist for *OneNewsNow*, a contributor to *World Magazine*, and a producer for CBS News), Marcia Segelstein has covered cultural and family issues for twenty-five years.

For the *National Catholic Register* Marcia writes a regular blog on cultural issues of interest to Catholic readers, especially parents. Her topics focus on raising Catholic kids in a secular world. For *Salvo* she writes a regular column called "Home Front," in which she tackles issues facing parents today, from pornography to sex education. For her "Person of Interest" column, Marcia interviews newsmakers on the cutting edge of the culture wars. Her interview subjects have included Lila Rose, Marjorie Dannenfelser, Eric Metaxas, Robert George, Cal Thomas, and Maggie Gallagher. In her feature pieces for *Salvo* she has covered topics including post-abortion healing, reviving the virtue of chastity before marriage, and how new family structures endanger children.

At CBS News, Marcia created, developed, and produced a family-issues feature that aired three times weekly on *CBS This Morning*. Prior to that, she was a Senior Producer on the CBS News Foreign Desk.

Marcia is a graduate of Georgetown University's School of Foreign Service. She lives in suburban New York City with her husband. They have two twenty-something children.

ACKNOWLEDGMENTS

I'll be forever grateful to Mary Beth Baker at OSV for her kindness, graciousness, patience, and wisdom in guiding me through the process of writing this book. I want to thank Marybeth Hicks for showing me how to put together a book proposal and for helping me figure out what I wanted to write. Thanks also to my editors over the years, especially Jim Kushiner at *Salvo* magazine and Kevin Knight at *National Catholic Register* for giving me the opportunity to write. Most of all I thank my husband and my children for their love, support, and prayers. You are precious gifts from God and the loves of my life.

NOTES

1. Dr. Jane Anderson, quoted in Marcia Segelstein, "Are Modern Parents Afraid to be Authority Figures?" *National Catholic Register*, September 15, 2017, http://www.ncregister.com/blog/segelstein/are-modern-parents-afraid-to-be-authority-figures.

2. "Diana Baumrind's (1966) Prototypical Descriptions of 3 Parenting Styles," devpsy.org, accessed February 5, 2019, http://www.devpsy.org/teaching/parent/baumrind_styles.html.

3. Dr. Veritas, "Love, Limits, and Latitude: Authoritative Parenting (pt. 1)," American College of Pediatricians, May 29, 2017, https://www.acpeds.org/love-limits-and-latitude-authoritative-parenting-pt-1.

4. William Doherty, *Take Back Your Kids: Confident Parenting in Turbulent Times* (Notre Dame: Sorin Books, 2000), 23.

5. Ibid.

6. Ron Taffel, *Childhood Unbound: Authoritative Parenting for the 21st Century* (New York: Free Press, 2010), 26.

7. Marcia Segelstein, "Are Modern Parents Afraid to be Authority Figures?" *National Catholic Register*, September 15, 2017, http://www.ncregister.com/blog/segelstein/are-modern-parents-afraid-to-be-authority-figures.

8. William Doherty, quoted in Marcia Segelstein, "No Fault Kids," *Salvo* magazine, no. 13 (Summer 2010), http://www.salvomag.com/new/articles/salvo13/13segelstein.php.

9. Ibid.

10. Leonard Sax, *The Collapse of Parenting: How We Hurt Our Kids When We Treat Them Like Grown-Ups* (New York: Basic Books, 2016), 30.

11. Taffel, *Childhood Unbound: Authoritative Parenting for the 21st Century*, 23.

12. Ibid., 26.

13. Ibid., 39–40.

14. Doherty: *Take Back Your Kids*, 13–14.

15. Taffel, *Childhood Unbound*, 26.

16. Doherty, *Take Back Your Kids*, 24.

17. Dr. Kathleen Kline, quoted in Marcia Segelstein, "No Fault Kids," *Salvo* magazine, no. 13 (Summer 2010), http://www.salvomag.com/new/articles/salvo13/13segelstein.php.

18. Ibid.

19. Taffel, *Childhood Unbound*, 12.

20. Commission on Children at Risk, *Hardwired to Connect: The New Scientific Case for Authoritative Communities* (New York: Institute for American Values, 2003), 33–36.

21. Sax, *The Collapse of Parenting*, 29.

22. Ibid., 113.

23. Ibid., 112.

24. Segelstein, "Are Modern Parents Afraid to be Authority Figures?"

25. Marcia Segelstein, "Has Discipline Become a Dirty Word?" *National Catholic Register*, October 14, 2017, http://www.ncregister.com/blog/segelstein/has-discipline-become-a-dirty-word.

26. Dr. Thomas Lickona, *How to Raise Kind Kids and Get Respect, Gratitude, and a Happier Family in the Bargain* (New York: Penguin Books, 2018), 103.

27. Dr. Veritas, "10 Basic Principles of Good Parenting – Part 3," American College of Pediatricians, August 15, 2016, https://www.acpeds.org/10-basic-principles-of-good-parenting-part-3?highlight=rules.

28. Segelstein, "Are Modern Parents Afraid to be Authority Figures?"

29. "The Benefits of the Family Table," American College of Pediatricians, May 2014, https://www.acpeds.org/the-college-speaks/position-statements/parenting-issues/the-benefits-of-the-family-table.

30. Ibid.

31. Ibid.

32. Doherty, *Take Back Your Kids*, 48.

33. Lickona, *How to Raise Kind Kids*, 42–43.

34. Ibid., 135.

35. Samuel Smith, "School District Refuses to Share LGBT Videos With Parents After Students Forced to Watch," Christian Post, July 2, 2018, https://www.christianpost.com/news/school-district-refuses-to-share-lgbt-videos-with-parents-after-students-

were-forced-to-watch-225627/.

36. John Stonestreet and Roberto Rivera, "Breakpoint: Gender Ideology and Public Schools," Breakpoint, May 16, 2018, http://www.breakpoint.org/2018/05/breakpoint-gender-ideology-public-schools/.

37. Ibid.

38. Ibid.

39. Ibid.

40. Jessica Herthel and Jazz Jennings, *I Am Jazz* (New York: Penguin Random House, 2014).

41. Dr. Michelle Cretella, quoted in Marcia Segelstein, "What if Your Child is 'Gender Confused'?" *National Catholic Register*, July 13, 2017, http://www.ncregister.com/blog/segelstein/what-if-your-child-is-gender-confused.

42. Ibid.

43. Walt Heyer, "I Used to Be Transgender. Here's My Take on Kids Who Think They Are Transgender," The Daily Signal, February 16, 2106, https://www.dailysignal.com/2016/02/16/i-used-to-be-transgender-heres-my-take-on-kids-who-think-they-are-transgender/.

44. Claire Chretien, "Minnesota parents sue school for refusing to teach 5-year-olds about transgenderism," LifeSiteNews, April 26, 2016, https://www.lifesitenews.com/news/minnesota-parents-sue-school-for-refusing-to-teach-five-year-olds-about-tra.

45. D. C. McAllister, "Minnesota Parents Sue To Get Trans Classes In Kindergarten," The Federalist, April 25, 2016, http://thefederalist.com/2016/04/25/minnesota-parents-sue-to-get-trans-classes-in-kindergarten/.

46. "Nebraska Bishops' Statement on the Nebraska School Activities Association's Policy on Transgender Student Participation," statement of the Catholic Diocese of Lincoln, January 4, 2016, https://www.lincolndiocese.org/bishops/bishop-james-conley/statements/4168-statement-on-the-nsaa-transgender-policy.

47. Bradford Richardson, "Pro-family group director: Rocklin Academy's transgender lesson plan led to enrollment drop," *Washington Times*, September 21, 2017, https://www.washingtontimes.com/news/2017/sep/21/karen-england-rocklin-academys-transgender-lesson-/.

48. "'I Can Now Say It': Elementary School Principal Comes Out As Transgender," CBS Boston, February 7, 2018, https://boston.cbslocal.com/2018/02/07/swampscott-elementry-school-principal-transgender-announcement/.

49. Michael F. Haverluck, "Maine schools trash parental rights for transgender policy," NE News Now, December 3, 2017, https://www.onenewsnow.com/education/2017/12/03/maine-schools-trash-parental-rights-for-transgender-policy.

50. Paul S. Coakley, "Archbishop of OKC: It's about more than restrooms," Catholics for America, May 29, 2016, http://catholicsforamerica.org/archbishop-of-okc-its-about-more-than-restrooms/.

51. Letter to parents from Sisters of Mercy of the Americas, May 11, 2016, available at https://www.scribd.com/doc/312408489/Letter-to-parents-of-San-Francisco-s-Mercy-High-School-students-released-May-11.

52. Daniel Guernsey, "Transgender Teachers in Catholic Schools?" *Crisis Magazine*, June 2, 2016, https://www.crisismagazine.com/2016/transgender-teachers-catholic-schools.

53. Rodney Pelletier, "Pope Francis Blasts Gender Ideology," ChurchMilitant.com, October 6, 2017, https://www.churchmilitant.com/news/article/pope-francis-blasts-gender-ideology.

54. Guernsey, "Transgender Teachers in Catholic Schools?"

55. Pete Baklinski, "WATCH: We must proclaim the 'truth about the conjugal union' to renew Christian culture, says Cardinal Burke," LifeSiteNews, June 6, 2016, https://www.lifesitenews.com/news/watch-we-must-proclaim-the-truth-about-the-conjugal-union-to-renew-christia.

56. Dustin Siggins, "School district votes to allow teachers to give condoms to students without parental consent," LifeSiteNews, June 4, 2014, https://www.lifesitenews.com/news/school-district-votes-to-allow-teachers-to-give-condoms-to-students-without.

57. Anna Gorman, "Unusual partnership offers students birth control," *Los Angeles Times*, June 5, 2012, http://articles.latimes.com/2012/jun/05/local/la-me-planned-parenthood-20120605.

58. "MassResistance hammers Education Committee at public hearing on 'student survey' bill," MassResistance, May 10, 2015, https://www.massresistance.org/docs/gen2/15b/School-surveys/hearing_050615.html.

59. "2015 National Youth Risk Behavior Survey," MassResistance, accessed February 4, 2019, https://www.massresistance.org/docs/gen2/15b/School-surveys/2015-CHS-YRBS-questionnaire.pdf.

60. Stephen A. Paparo, Ph.D., "The ABCs of Creating an LGBTQ-Friendly Classroom," *Massachusetts Music Educators Journal* 64, no. 3 (Spring 2016): 37–39, https://www.massresistance.org

/docs/gen3/16b/lgbt-music-classes/images/general-music-mag.pdf.

61. Peter Holley, "Parent furious eighth-grader's homework had question about contracting herpes from 'one night stand,'" *Washington Post*, November 7, 2015, https://www.washingtonpost.com/news/morning-mix/wp/2015/11/07/parents-furious-eighth-graders-homework-had-question-about-contracting-herpes-from-one-night-stand/?noredirect=on&utm_term=.cc15c4b31414.

62. Todd Starnes, "Students opposed to LGBT agenda shamed in classroom," FOX News, February 9, 2015, https://www.foxnews.com/opinion/students-opposed-to-lgbt-agenda-shamed-in-classroom.

63. Pacific Justice Institute, "SF Bay Area School Permits Queer Straight Alliance to Bully Students," February 5, 2015, https://www.pacificjustice.org/press-releases/sf-bay-area-school-permits-queer-straight-alliance-to-bully-students.

64. Starnes, "Students opposed to LGBT agenda shamed in classroom."

65. "Cardinal Burke: Catholic Education Must Transmit the Unbroken Tradition," address delivered at the Voice of the Family press conference in Rome, October 15, 2015, http://voiceofthefamily.com/cardinal-burke-catholic-education-must-transmit-the-unbroken-tradition/.

66. *Compendium of the Catechism of the Catholic Church*, 460.

67. Sabrina Arena Ferrisi, "How to Raise Devoted Catholic Kids When They Attend Public School," *National Catholic Register*, February 20, 2018, http://www.ncregister.com/daily-news/how-to-raise-devoted-catholic-kids-when-they-attend-public-school.

68. Focus on the Family, "Christian Parents Uncomfortable With School's 'Diversity Training,'" Family Q&A, accessed February 4, 2019, https://www.focusonthefamily.com/family-q-and-a/parenting/christian-parents-uncomfortable-with-schools-diversity-training.

69. Denise Donohue and Dan Guernsey, "Choosing a Catholic School Begins with Mission," *National Catholic Register*, January 30, 2018, http://www.ncregister.com/blog/guest-blogger/choosing-a-catholic-school-begins-with-mission.

70. "Parent Guide," The Cardinal Newman Society, accessed February 4, 2019, https://newmansociety.org/principles-catholic-identity-education/parent-guide/.

71. US Conference of Catholic Bishops, "Catholic Education," USCCB, accessed February 5, 2019, http://www.usccb.org/beliefs-and-teachings/how-we-teach/catholic-education/

upload/2013-By-the-Numbers-Catholic-Education.pdf.

72. Brian D. Ray, Ph.D., "Research Facts on Homeschooling," National Home Education Research Institute (NHERI), January 13, 2018, https://www.nheri.org/research-facts-on-homeschooling/.

73. https://www.rcahybrid.org/, accessed February 5, 2019.

74. https://hlsda.org, accessed February 5, 2019.

75. Mary Kay Clark, "Catholic Home Schooling," EWTN, accessed February 4, 2019, https://www.ewtn.com/library/ HOMESCHL/CATHHS.HTM.

76. "The Impact of Media Use and Screen Time on Children, Adolescents, and Families," American College of Pediatricians, November 2016, https://www.acpeds.org/the-college-speaks/ position-statements/parenting-issues/the-impact-of-media-use-and-screen-time-on-children-adolescents-and-families.

77. The Henry J. Kaiser Family Foundation, "Generation M^2: Media in the Lives of 8- to 18-Year-Olds," https:// kaiserfamilyfoundation.files.wordpress.com/2013/01/8010.pdf; see also http://www.pewinternet.org/2018/05/31/teens-social-media-technology-2018/.

78. "New Research by Common Sense Finds Major Spike in Mobile Media Use and Device Ownership by Children Age 0 to 8," Common Sense Media, October 19, 2017, https://www. commonsensemedia.org/about-us/news/press-releases/new-research-by-common-sense-finds-major-spike-in-mobile-media-use-and.

79. "The Impact of Media Use and Screen Time on Children, Adolescents, and Families."

80. American Academy of Pediatrics, Council on Communications and Media, "Children, Adolescents, and the Media," *Pediatrics* 132, no. 5 (November 2013), http://pediatrics.aappublications.org/ content/132/5/958.

81. "The Impact of Media Use and Screen Time on Children, Adolescents, and Families."

82. Jean Twenge, "New findings add twist to screen time limit debate," The Conversation, November 6, 2018, updated November 13, 2018, http://theconversation.com/new-findings-add-twist-to-screen-time-limit-debate-105717.

83. Kyla Boyse, RN, "Television and Children," University of Michigan Medicine, updated August 2010, http://www.med.umich. edu/yourchild/topics/tv.

84. Ibid.

85. Ibid.

86. "The Impact of Media Use and Screen Time on Children, Adolescents, and Families."

87. Monica Anderson and Jingjing Jiang, "Teens, Social Media & Technology 2018," Pew Research Center, May 31, 2018, http://www.pewinternet.org/2018/05/31/teens-social-media-technology-2018/.

88. Mark Lerner, quoted in Naomi Schaefer Riley, *Be the Parent, Please: Stop Banning Seesaws and Start Banning Snapchat* (West-Conshohocken, PA: Templeton Press, 2018), 86–87.

89. Jean Twenge, "Have Smartphones Destroyed a Generation?" *The Atlantic*, September 2017, https://www.theatlantic.com/magazine/archive/2017/09/has-the-smartphone-destroyed-a-generation/534198/.

90. John Stonestreet and G. Shane Morris, "BreakPoint: Delete Amino & Musical.ly," Breakpoint, April 2, 2018, http://www.breakpoint.org/2018/04/breakpoint-delete-amino-musical-ly/.

91. American College of Pediatricians, "Protecting Your Children on the Internet," Patient Information Handout, 2015, http://www.acpeds.org/wordpress/wp-content/uploads/9.16.15-B-Internet-Safety-Handout-with-live-streaming-and-FBI-resource.doc.

92. Leonard Sax, *Girls on the Edge: The Four Factors Driving the New Crisis for Girls—Sexual Identity, the Cyberbubble, Obsessions, Environmental Toxins* (New York: Basic Books, 2011), 39.

93. Twenge, "Have Smartphones Destroyed a Generation?"

94. Monica Anderson, "A Majority of Teens Have Experienced Some Form of Cyberbullying," Pew Research Center, September 27, 2018, http://www.pewinternet.org/2018/09/27/a-majority-of-teens-have-experienced-some-form-of-cyberbullying/.

95. Teensafe, "Everything a Parent Needs to Know About SNAPCHAT," TeenSafe, November 16, 2015, https://www.teensafe.com/blog/everything-a-parent-needs-to-know-about-snapchat/.

96. Wayne Parker, "Shapchat—a Popular App for Teens But With a Dark Side," Very Well Family, September 28, 2018, https://www.verywellfamily.com/what-is-snapchat-and-its-use-1270338.

97. Clive Thompson, "Clive Thompson on the Age of Microcelebrity: Why Everyone's a Little Brad Pitt," *Wired*, November 27, 2007, https://www.wired.com/2007/11/st-thompson/.

98. Sax, *Girls On The Edge: The Four Factors Driving the New Crisis for Girls*, 66.

99. Ibid., 188.

100. Ibid., 209.

101. Twenge, "Have Smartphones Destroyed a Generation?"

102. Nancy Jo Sales, *American Girls: Social Media and the Secret Lives of Teenagers* (New York: Penguin Random House, 2016), 42.

103. Sheri Madigan, Ph.D., Anh Ly, MA, Christina L. Rash, BA, et al., "Prevalence of Multiple Forms of Sexting Behavior Among Youth," *JAMA Pediatrics* 172, no. 4 (April 2018): 327–335, https://jamanetwork.com/journals/jamapediatrics/article-abstract/2673719.

104. Elizabeth Englander, Ph.D., and Meghan McCoy, EdD, "Sexting—Prevalence, Age, Sex, and Outcomes," *JAMA Pediatrics* 172, no. 4 (April 2018): 317–318, https://jamanetwork.com/journals/jamapediatrics/article-abstract/2673715.

105. Jonathan van Maren, "Parents, your teens are being pressured to 'sext.' Even at Christian high schools," LifeSiteNews, January 3, 2018, https://www.lifesitenews.com/blogs/parents-your-teens-are-being-pressured-to-sext.-even-at-christian-high-scho.

106. "The Impact of Media Use and Screen Time on Children, Adolescents, and Families."

107. Gigi Engle, "Anal Sex: What You Need to Know," *Teen Vogue*, May 16, 2018, https://www.teenvogue.com/story/anal-sex-what-you-need-to-know.

108. Melanie Mignucci, "Back to School Awards 2017: The Best Health and Wellness Products," *Teen Vogue*, June 1, 2017, https://www.teenvogue.com/gallery/back-to-school-awards-2017-health-wellness-products?verso=true.

109. Cardinal Robert Sarah, *The Power of Silence: Against the Dictatorship of Noise* (San Francisco: Ignatius Press, 2017), 22.

110. Ibid., 27.

111. Ibid., 25.

112. Melissa Henson, "Over-the-Top or a Race to the Bottom: A Parent's Guide to Streaming Video," Parents Television Council, accessed February 4, 2019, http://w2.parentstv.org/MediaFiles/PDF/Studies/OTT2017_D.pdf.

113. Rebecca Hagelin, *30 Ways in 30 Days to Save Your Family* (Washington, D.C.: Regnery Publishing, 2009), 155.

114. Nathan McAlone, "Young people spend about twice as much time watching Netflix as live TV, and even more time on YouTube," *Business Insider*, May 1, 2017, https://www.businessinsider.com/teens-watching-netflix-youtube-more-than-tv-2017-5.

115. "Gen Z: Leaders of the Mobile Social Movement," Awesomeness TV, accessed February 4, 2019, https://awesomenessty.

com/genz/.

116. Dr. Veritas, "Parental Controls," American College of Pediatricians, July 18, 2016, https://www.acpeds.org/parental-controls.

117. Betsy Morris, "Parents' Dilemma: When to Give Children Smartphones," *Wall Street Journal*, January 12, 2018, https://www.wsj.com/articles/iphones-vs-parents-the-tug-of-war-over-americas-children-1515772695.

118. Twenge, "Have Smartphones Destroyed a Generation?"

119. Neil J. Rubenking and Ben Moore, "The Best Parental Control Software of 2018," *PC Mag*, November 7, 2018, https://www.pcmag.com/article2/0,2817,2346997,00.asp.

120. Paul Wagenseil, "Best Parental-Control Apps of 2018," Tom's Guide, November 28, 2018, https://www.tomsguide.com/us/best-parental-control-apps,review-2258.html.

121. Stonestreet and Morris, "BreakPoint: Delete Amino & Musical.ly."

122. "A Parent's Guide to Amino Apps," Axis, 2018, https://axis.org/wp-content/uploads/2018/06/Axis-Parents-Guide-to-Amino-Apps.pdf.

123. Sax, *Girls On The Edge*, 54.

124. Stonestreet and Morris, "BreakPoint: Delete Amino & Musical.ly."

125. Father Dan Beeman, Twitter post, July 21, 2018, 7:15 a.m., https://twitter.com/inthelineofmel

126. Sax, *Girls On The Edge*, 64.

127. "The Impact of Media Use and Screen Time on Children, Adolescents, and Families."

128. Dr. Veritas, "Online Computer Game and Video Game Addictions," American College of Pediatricians, August 28, 2017, https://www.acpeds.org/online-computer-game-and-video-game-addictions.

129, Mark Regnerus, *Forbidden Fruit: Sex & Religion in the Lives of American Teenagers* (New York: Oxford University Press, 2007), 86–87.

130. Mark Regnerus and Jeremy Uecker, *Premarital Sex in America* (New York: Oxford University Press, 2011), 15.

131. Megan K. Beckett, Marc N. Elliott, Steven Martino, et al., "Timing of Parent and Child Communication About Sexuality Relative to Children's Sexual Behaviors," *Pediatrics 125*, no. 1 (January 2010), http://pediatrics.aappublications.org/content/125/1/34. short. See also, Ellen Friedrichs, "Here's How (and When) To Talk To Your Kids About Porn," Kveller, December 29, 2017, https://

www.kveller.com/sex-educator-heres-how-and-when-to-talk-to-your-kids-about-porn/.

132. Arina Grossu and Peter Sprigg, "Sexual Risk-Avoidance Education," Family Research Council, accessed February 5, 2019, https://www.frc.org/SexualRiskAvoidance.

133. Ascend, "Sexual Risk Avoidance Works," 2016, https://weascend.org/wp-content/uploads/2017/10/sraworksweb.pdf.

134. Advocates for Youth, accessed February 5, 2019, https://advocatesforyouth.org/about/our-legacy/.

135. Miriam Grossman, *You're Teaching My Child What?* (Washington, DC: Regnery Publishing, 2009), 23.

136. Ibid., 25–26.

137. Dr. Miriam Grossman, quoted in Marcia Segelstein, "Rotten Apple Awards: Sex Ed Based on Lies Is Child Abuse," *Salvo* magazine, no. 12 (Spring 2010), http://www.salvomag.com/new/articles/salvo12/12segelstein.php.

138. "Sex ed is a human right. It's time we start treating it like one," Sexuality Information and Education Council of the United States, accessed February 5. 2019, https://siecus.org/sex-ed-is-a-human-right-its-time-we-start-treating-it-like-one/.

139. National Guidelines Task Force, "Topic 1: Reproductive and Sexual Anatomy and Physiology," in "Key Concept 1: Human Development," in *Guidelines for Comprehensive Sexuality Education*, 3rd Edition, accessed February 5, 2019, http://sexedu.org.tw/guideline.pdf, 25.

140. Ibid., "Topic 3: Reproduction," 26.

141. Ibid., "Topic 5: Sexual Orientation," 29.

142. Ibid., "Topic 1: Families," in "Key Concept 2: Relationships," 33.

143. Ibid., "Topic 5: Marriage and Lifetime Commitments," 39.

144. Ibid.

145. Ibid., "Topic 2: Masturbation," in "Key Concept 4: Sexual Behavior," 51.

146. Ibid., "Topic 5: Sexual Orientation," 29.

147. Ibid., "Topic 1: Families," in "Key Concept 2: Relationships," 34.

148. Ibid., "Topic 2: Masturbation," in "Key Concept 4: Sexual Behavior," 34.

149. Ibid., "Topic 4: Abortion," in "Key Concept 5: Sexual Health," 60.

150. Ibid., "Topic 5: Sexual Orientation," in "Key Concept 1:

Human Development," 30.

151. Ibid., "Topic 6: Gender Identity," in "Key Concept 1: Human Development," 31.

152. Ibid., "Topic 1: Values," in "Key Concept 3: Personal Skills," 43.

153. Ibid.

154. Ibid., "Topic 2: Masturbation," in "Key Concept 4: Sexual Behavior," 52.

155. Ibid., "Topic 3: Shared Sexual Behavior," in "Key Concept 4: Sexual Behavior," 53.

156. Ibid., "Topic 2: Contraception," in "Key Concept 5: Sexual Health," 59.

157. Ibid.

158. Ibid., "Topic 1: Sexuality and Society," in "Key Concept 6: Society and Culture," 71.

159. Ibid., "Topic 1: Sexuality Throughout Life," in "Key Concept 4: Sexual Behavior," 51.

160. Ibid., "Topic 6: Gender Identity," in "Key Concept 1: Human Development," 32.

161. Ibid., "Topic 5: Human Sexual Response," in "Key Concept 4: Sexual Behavior," 55.

162. Ibid., "Topic 6: Sexual Fantasy," in "Key Concept 4: Sexual Behavior," 56.

163. Ibid., "Topic 4: Sexuality and Religion," in "Key Concept 6: Society and Culture," 74.

164. "Sexual Risk Behaviors: HIV, STD, & Teen Pregnancy Prevention," CDC, Adolescent and School Health, accessed February 5, 2019, https://www.cdc.gov/healthyyouth/sexualbehaviors/.

165. Helen Branswell, "HPV a risk even with one partner, study finds," *The Star*, January 13, 2008, https://www.thestar.com/life/health_wellness/2008/01/13/hpv_a_risk_even_with_one_partner_study_finds.html.

166. "Human Papillomavirus (HPV) Vaccines," Cancer.gov, accessed February 5, 2019, https://www.cancer.gov/about-cancer/causes-prevention/risk/infectious-agents/hpv-vaccine-fact-sheet.

167 Y. S. Marfatia, Ipsa Pandya, and Kajal Mehta, "Condoms: Past, present, and future," National Center for Biotechnology Information (NCBI), accessed February 5, 2019, https://www.ncbi.nlm.nih.gov/pmc/articles/PMC4660551/.

168. Miriam Grossman, *Unprotected: A Campus Psychiatrist Reveals How Political Correctness in Her Profession Endangers Every Student* (New York: Sentinel, 2007), 12.

169. Kristen Walker Hatten, "Hi, my name is Kristen, and I'm abstinent," LifeSiteNews, February 27, 2012, https://www. lifesitenews.com/opinion/hi-my-name-is-kristen-and-im-abstinent.

170. John Stonestreet and Brett Kunkle, *A Practical Guide to Culture: Helping the Next Generation Navigate Today's World* (Colorado Springs: David C. Cook, 2017), 174.

171. Linda Klepacki, "Before the Talk Dealing With Our Past," Focus on the Family, 2004, accessed February 6, 2019, https://www.focusonthefamily.com/parenting/sexuality/talking-about-sex/before-the-talk-dealing-with-our-past.

172. "Induced Abortion in the United States," Guttmacher Institute, January 2018, https://www.guttmacher.org/fact-sheet/induced-abortion-united-states.

173. Ibid.

174. Theresa Burke's story, and the stories of the other women in this section (Cynthia, Michaelene, and Jennifer O'Neill), were originally published in Marcia Segelstein, "A Buried Grief: Finally, There Is More Help for Women Hurt by Abortion," *Salvo* magazine, no. 14 (Autumn 2010), http://www.salvomag.com/new/articles/salvo14/14segelstein.php.

175. Planned Parenthood, answer to "How will I feel after my abortion?" in "What can I expect after having an in-clinic abortion?", accessed November 7, 2018, https://www.plannedparenthood.org/learn/abortion/in-clinic-abortion-procedures/what-can-i-expect-after-having-an-in-clinic-abortion.

176. David Shaw, quoted in Bernard Goldberg, *Arrogance: Rescuing America from the Media Elite* (New York: Mediumcool Inc., 2003), 136.

177. American Psychological Association, "Executive Summary of the Task Force Report," in *Mental Health and Abortion*, accessed February 5, 2019, https://www.apa.org/pi/women/programs/abortion/.

178. "Induced Abortion and Mental Health," Academy of Medical Royal Colleges, December 2011, https://www.aomrc.org.uk/wp-content/uploads/2016/05/Induced_Abortion_Mental_Health_1211.pdf.

179. Segelstein, "A Buried Grief: Finally, There Is More Help for Women Hurt by Abortion."

180. Terrell Clemmons, "Men, Abortion & Hemingway," *Salvo* magazine, no. 21 (Summer 2012), http://salvomag.com/new/articles/salvo21/harms-way-men-abortion-hemingway.php.

181. Catherine T. Coyle and Vincent M. Rue, "Men's Mental Health and Abortion: A Review of the Research," in *UFL Life and Learning Conference XXVII*, 261–76. Available at http://www.uffl. org/pdfs/vol27/UFL_2017_Coyle.pdf.

182. "Men & Abortion," Rachel's Vineyard, accessed February 5, 2019, http://www.rachelsvineyard.org/men/testimonies.aspx.

183. Ascend: How to Bring Sexual Risk Avoidance Education to Your School, Parents School Toolkit, accessed February 5, 2019, https://weascend.org/wp-content/uploads/2017/10/ascendparentss-chooltoolkit-min.pdf.

184. Conversation with Valerie Huber originally published in Marcia Segelstein, "Sex Re-education: A Parent's Guide to Sex Ed," *Salvo* magazine, no. 29 (Summer 2014), http://www.salvomag. com/new/articles/salvo29/sex-reeducation.php.

185. "Sexual Risk Avoidance Education: What You Need To Know," Ascend, https://weascend.org/wp-content/uploads/ 2018/01/Sexual-Risk-Avoidance-Education-What-You-Need-to-Know.pdf?x69289.

186. Peter Kreeft, *Because God Is Real* (San Francisco: Ignatius Press, 2008), 139.

187. Rebecca Smith, "The Thrill of the Chaste," Catholic Exchange, June 25, 2015, https://catholicexchange.com/the-thrill-of-the-chaste.

188. W. Knight, "How is chastity better? Let me count the ways," in "Facing Chastity," *Salvo* magazine, no. 21 (Summer 2012), http://salvomag.com/new/articles/salvo21/facing-chastity-the-unpopular-virtue.php.

189. Dr. Michael Artigues, quoted in Marcia Segelstein, "How to Talk to Your Kids About Sex in a Sex-Obsessed Culture," *National Catholic Register*, January 30, 2018, http://www.ncregister. com/blog/segelstein/how-to-talk-to-your-kids-about-sex-in-a-sex-obsessed-culture.

190. Brigham Young University, "Couples who delay having sex get benefits later, study suggests," Science Daily, December 29, 2010, https://www.sciencedaily.com/releases/2010/12/ 101222112102.htm.

191. Dr. Jenell Williams Paris, quoted in Tyler Charles, "(Almost) Everyone's Doing It," *Relevant* magazine, no. 53 (September/ October 2011), 65–69.

192. Mark Regnerus, quoted in Marcia Segelstein, "Intercourse Correction: The Devaluation of Chastity Before Marriage & How It Might Be Recovered," *Salvo* magazine, no. 16 (Spring

2011), http://www.salvomag.com/new/articles/salvo16/16segelstein. php.

193. "The Law: Clearing the Calendar," *Time*, July 8, 1974, http://content.time.com/time/subscriber/article/0,33009,943928,00. html.

194. Committee on Laity, Marriage, Family Life and Youth, "Create in Me a Clean Heart: A Pastoral Response to Pornography," US Conference of Catholic Bishops (USCCB), 2015, http://www.usccb.org/issues-and-action/human-life-and-dignity/pornography/upload/Create-in-Me-a-Clean-Heart-Statement-on-Pornography.pdf, 13.

195. David Kinnaman, "The Porn Phenomenon," Barna, February 5, 2016, https://www.barna.com/the-porn-phenomenon/.

196. Judith Reisman, *"Soft Porn" Plays Hardball* (Lafayette, LA: Huntington House Publishers, 1991), 9.

197. "Technical report of the Commission on Obscenity and Pornography," accessed February 5, 2019, https://catalog.hathitrust. org/Record/009911547.

198. Aaron Hass, *Teenage Sexuality* (New York: Scribner, 1979), 184.

199. Mary Anne Layden, *The Social Costs of Pornography* (Princeton, NJ: Witherspoon Institute, 2010).

200. "Pornography," Marriage and Religion Research Institute (MARRI), March 8, 2018, http://marri.us/a-world-wide-public-health-family-health-pandemic/.

201. Jill Manning, *What's the Big Deal About Pornography: A Guide for the Internet Generation* (Salt Lake City: Shadow Mountain, 2008).

202. Committee on Laity, Marriage, Family Life and Youth, "Create in Me a Clean Heart: A Pastoral Response to Pornography,"

203. Dr. Jill Manning, quoted in Marcia Segelstein, "Blindsided Kids," *Salvo* magazine, no. 9 (Summer 2009), http://www.salvomag.com/new/articles/salvo9/9segelstein.php.

204. Michael Flood, "The harms of pornography exposure among children and young people," Wiley Online Library, November 2, 2009, https://onlinelibrary.wiley.com/doi/abs/10.1002/car.1092.

205. "The Impact of Pornography on Children," American College of Pediatricians, June 2016, https://www.acpeds.org/the-college-speaks/position-statements/the-impact-of-pornography-on-children.

206. Enough Is Enough, "Statistics by Category," accessed February 5, 2019, https://enough.org/stats_youth_and_porn_archives.

207. Daniel Schwartz, "Sexting, pornography findings in youth survey a new warning," CBC News, May 29, 2014, https://www.cbc.ca/news/health/sexting-pornography-findings-in-youth-survey-a-new-warning-1.2657708.

208. Janis Wolak, Kimberly Mitchell, and David Finkelhor, "Unwanted and Wanted Exposure to Online Pornography in a National Sample of Youth Internet Users," *Pediatrics* 119, no. 2 (February 2007), http://pediatrics.aappublications.org/content/119/2/247.short.

209. "Pornography Statistics," Covenant Eyes, accessed February 5, 2019, https://www.covenanteyes.com/pornstats/.

210. EIE, Statistics by Category.

211. MARRI, "Pornography."

212. GuardChild, "Internet Statistics," accessed February 5, 2019, https://www.guardchild.com/statistics/.

213. Manning, *What's the Big Deal About Pornography.*

214. "Norman Doidge on pornography and neuroplasticity: 'The Brain That Changes Itself,' (2007)," Your Brain on Porn, accessed February 6, 2019, https://www.yourbrainonporn.com/relevant-research-and-articles-about-the-studies/porn-use-sex-addiction-studies/norman-doidge-on-pornography-and-neuroplasticity-the-brain-that-changes-itself-2007/.

215. Committee on Laity, Marriage, Family Life and Youth, "Create in Me a Clean Heart," 13.

216. Christine Sanderson, *The Seduction of Children* (London: Jessica Kingsley Publishers, 2004), 129.

217. Internet Safety 101, "Pornography 101," accessed February 5, 2019, https://internetsafety101.org/whatispornography.

218. Amanda Lenhart, "Protecting Teens Online," Pew Research Center, March 17, 2005, http://www.pewinternet.org/2005/03/17/protecting-teens-online/.

219. Monica Anderson, "Parents, Teens and Digital Monitoring," Pew Research Center, January 7, 2016, http://www.pewinternet.org/2016/01/07/parents-teens-and-digital-monitoring/.

220. Internet Safety 101, a program of Enough Is Enough, accessed February 5, 2019, https://internetsafety101.org/internetsafety101.

221. Manning quoted in Segelstein, "Blindsided Kids."

222. See James Dirksen's comments in Marcia Segelstein, "Porn Blockers: A Primer for Parents," *Salvo* magazine, no. 28 (Spring 2014), http://salvomag.com/new/articles/salvo28/porn-blockers.php.

223. Educate and Empower Kids, *How To Talk to Your Kids About Pornography* (Bourne, TX: Educate and Empower Kids, 2016), 8.

224. Ibid.

225. Courtney Cagle, "Safe and Savvy: The Best Internet and Phone Filters of 2018," Educate and Empower Kids, accessed February 8, 2019, https://educateempowerkids.org/safe-savvy-best-internet-phone-filters-2018.

226. Segelstein, "Porn Blockers."

227. MARRI, "Pornography."

228. Pope Francis, Homily, September 29, 2013, St. Peter's Square, text available at http://w2.vatican.va/content/francesco/en/homilies/2013/documents/papa-francesco_20130929_giornata-catechisti.html.

229. Mark Whitehouse, "Number of the Week: Americans Buy More Stuff They Don't Need," *Wall Street Journal*, April 23, 2011, https://blogs.wsj.com/economics/2011/04/23/number-of-the-week-americans-buy-more-stuff-they-dont-need/.

230. John De Graaf, David Wann, Thomas Nayor, *Affluenza: How Overconsumption Is Killing Us – and How to Fight Back* (Oakland: Berrett-Koehler Publishers, 2014), 15.

231. Ibid., 49.

232. John Stonestreet and Brett Kunkle, *A Practical Guide to Culture: Helping the Next Generation Navigate Today's World* (Colorado Springs: David C. Cook, 2017), 228.

233. Christian Smith, Kari Christofferson, Hilary Davidson, *Lost in Transition: The Dark Side of Emerging Adulthood* (New York: Oxford University Press, 2011), 104.

234. Madeline Levine, Ph.D., *The Price of Privilege: How Parental Pressure and Material Advantage Are Creating a Generation of Disconnected and Unhappy Kids* (New York: HarperCollins, 2006), 17.

235. Ibid.

236. Doherty, *Take Back Your Kids*, 152.

237. Ibid., 153.

238. Paloma Kubiak, "Parents: do you succumb to pressure to keep up with the Joneses?" YourMoney.com, May 8, 2016, https://www.yourmoney.com/household-bills/parents-succumb-pressure-keep-joneses/.

239. Anna R. McAlister and T. Bettina Cornwell, "Children's Brand Symbolism Understanding: Links to Theory of Mind and Executive Functioning," *Psychology & Marketing* 27, no. 3 (March 2010): 224, https://deepblue.lib.umich.edu/bitstream/handle/2027.42/65039/20328_ftp.pdf?sequence=1.

240. Ibid., 150–151.

241. Campaign for a Commercial-Free Childhood, "Marketing to Children Overview," CCFC, accessed February 5, 2019, https://www.commercialfreechildhood.org/resource/marketing-children-overview.

242. Dr. Thomas Lickona, quoted in Marcia Segelstein, "How to Raise Good Kids in a Culture of Consumerism," *National Catholic Register*, December 22, 2017, http://www.ncregister.com/blog/segelstein/how-to-raise-good-kids-in-a-culture-of-consumerism.

243. Ibid.

244. Campaign for a Commercial-Free Childhood, "Marketing to Children Overview."

245. Rebecca Hagelin, *30 Ways in 30 Days to Save Your Family* (Washington, D.C.: Regnery Publishing, 2009), 218–219.

246. Lickona, quoted in Segelstein, "How to Raise Good Kids in a Culture of Consumerism."

247. Michele Borba, "6 Ways to 'Deprogram' a Materialistic Kid," *U.S. News & World Report*, February 24, 2017, https://health.usnews.com/wellness/for-parents/articles/2017-02-24/6-ways-to-deprogram-a-materialistic-kid.

248. Stonestreet and Kunkle, *A Practical Guide to Culture*, 233–234.

249. Lickona, quoted in Segelstein, "How to Raise Good Kids in a Culture of Consumerism."

250. Thomas Lickona, Ph.D., and Katie Hintz-Zambrano, "How to Raise Thankful Kids," *Mother* magazine, November 1, 2017, http://www.mothermag.com/how-to-raise-thankful-kids/.

251. Lickona, quoted in Segelstein, "How to Raise Good Kids in a Culture of Consumerism."

252. Hagelin, *30 Ways in 30 Days to Save Your Family*, 216–217.

253. Ibid., 217.

254. Lickona, quoted in Segelstein, "How to Raise Good Kids in a Culture of Consumerism."

255. Borba, "6 Ways to 'Deprogram' a Materialistic Kid."

256. Lickona, quoted in Segelstein, "How to Raise Good Kids in a Culture of Consumerism."

257. Dr. Veritas, "3 Ways to Help Your Kids Give Back on

#GivingTuesday," American College of Pediatricians, November 27, 2017, https://www.acpeds.org/3-ways-to-help-your-kids-give-back-on-givingtuesday.

258. Peter Kreeft, *Before I Go* (Lanham, MD: Sheed & Ward, 2007), 8.

259. Ibid., 11.

260. Ibid., 22.

261. See their website, familyformation.net.

262. United States Conference of Catholic Bishops, "Tools for Building a Domestic Church," USCCB.org, http://www.usccb.org/beliefs-and-teachings/vocations/parents/tools-for-building-a-domestic-church.cfm.

263. Cory Busse, "10 Things That Make for a Great Catholic Dad," pamphlet (Huntington, IN: Our Sunday Visitor, 2009). See also Cory Busse, "10 ways to be a great Catholic dad," *Our Sunday Visitor Newsweekly*, June 10, 2009, https://www.osv.com/OSVNewsweekly/ByIssue/Article/TabId/735/ArtMID/13636/ArticleID/413/10-ways-to-be-a-great-Catholic-dad.aspx.

264. "Praying Together As a Family," Focus on the Family, accessed February 5, 2019, https://www.focusonthefamily.com/family-q-and-a/parenting/praying-together-as-a-family.

265. Sarah Jennings, "Rebecca Hagelin on Raising Kids in a Culture Gone Mad," Crosswalk.com, April 19, 2005, https://www.crosswalk.com/family/parenting/rebecca-hagelin-on-raising-kids-in-a-culture-gone-mad-1325469.html.

266. Sabrina Arena Ferrisi, "How to Raise Devoted Catholic Kids When They Attend Public School," *National Catholic Register*, February 20, 2018, http://www.ncregister.com/daily-news/how-to-raise-devoted-catholic-kids-when-they-attend-public-school.

267. "The 25 Most Amazing Christian Summer Camps," Theology Degrees, accessed February 5, 2019, https://www.theologydegrees.org/features/the-25-most-amazing-christian-summer-camps/.

268. United States Conference of Catholic Bishops, "Tools for Building a Domestic Church."